Discovering Christ

An Inquiry and Meditation

Msgr. Francis D. Kelly

Discovering Christ

An Inquiry and Meditation

Msgr. Francis D. Kelly

WIPF & STOCK · Eugene, Oregon

Wipf and Stock Publishers
199 W 8th Ave, Suite 3
Eugene, OR 97401

Discovering Chirst
An Inquiry and Meditation
By Kelly, Francis D.
Copyright©2007 by Kelly, Francis D.
ISBN 13: 978-1-5326-1518-4
Publication date 12/5/2016
Previously published by Our Sunday Visitor, 2007

CONTENTS

INTRODUCTION

The contents of this book are the result of many years of reflection, meditation, and research on the mystery of Our Lord, Jesus Christ — some of it in connection with teaching Christology for thirteen years. It is offered with the conviction, expressed so clearly by our Holy Father, Pope Benedict XVI, in a sermon given shortly before he become Pope, that "Christianity is not an intellectual system, a packet of dogmas, a moralism. Christianity is rather an encounter, a love story; it is an event." This event is the "Christ Event."

In inviting the reader to "discover Jesus," I hope that in some small way that personal "encounter" with him can be facilitated or deepened, that love story can become also the reader's, as it has been the author's. Only Jesus Christ can give meaning to the whole of life — to this earthly pilgrimage and to eternity.

I, the author, make no claim to great originality. As the reader will see, I have been enriched by the insights and writings of many. Hopefully, however, this systematic arrangement and ordering of these insights will be useful to others in their effort to discover Jesus and welcome into their lives the peace, love, and joy he brings.

Many topics only touched upon here deserve fuller treatment. The footnotes will help the reader who wishes to further explore these issues. It is the author's conviction that a synthetic overall view of the mystery of Jesus would be the best service to many and hopefully motivate them to further contemplation, reading, and study, for "Jesus Christ is the same yesterday and today and for ever" (Heb. 13:8).

Recent popular books and movies have presented as historical fact allegations about Christology that are patently erroneous and even slanderous. Many persons with little Scriptural, theological, or historical understanding of their faith have been confused or deceived. All this indicates the need for a mature, factual, adult understanding of the truth about Christ. Hopefully, this book will make a contribution to that goal.

On a personal note, on my ordination card more than forty years ago I used the words of St. Paul as I began my own priestly ministry: "For what we preach is not ourselves, but Jesus Christ as Lord, with ourselves as your servants for Jesus' sake" (2 Cor. 4:5). I pray that this small book may be another expression of that desire, and so I offer it to Mary who first brought Christ to the world that she may help us to give birth to him anew in our hearts by living faith.

I am especially grateful to Avery Cardinal Dulles, S.J., Fr. Gerald O'Collins, S.J., and Fr. Alfred McBride, O.Praem, for reading the manuscript and making valuable suggestions, and to Elizabeth Segatori for help with the word processing of the text.

MSGR. FRANCIS D. KELLY

CHAPTER 1

A PERSONAL CHRISTOLOGY: WHO IS JESUS FOR ME?

In our faith journey, each person develops personal impressions or images of Jesus that emerge through life experience, catechetical training, retreats, reading, liturgy, and spiritual direction. As we move on in our journey with the Lord, these images develop and perhaps change, but they give personal focus to our prayer and our discipleship in a way that is meaningful to us.

It is useful at the beginning of this systematic exploration of the person and mystery of Jesus to be more consciously aware of our own personal Christology: who Jesus is for me now. This includes asking ourselves, "How does my personal approach to Jesus affect my thoughts, the movements of my heart, my behavior, my choices?"

Our search might well be inspired by these questions posed by the late, great Pope John Paul II in an address:

"Who is Jesus for me? Who is he really for my thoughts, for my heart, for my behavior? How do I

know him whom I confess? How do I speak about
him to others? Do I bear witness to him? How?"
(December 14, 1980)

Exploring one's personal Chistology helps one understand that a relationship to Jesus is never a matter of the
mind or intellect alone. It is a reality that involves the heart,
spirit, will, and intellect, a reality suffused by the grace of
God that alone ultimately enables us to have a proper understanding of and relationship to the Lord Jesus. "No one can
come to me unless the Father who sent me draws him" (Jn.
6:44).

God may use many elements as the instruments of his
grace: a good sermon, a helpful book or article, the sharing
of a friend, the impact of life experiences. All of these can
be means by which we are drawn deeper into a relationship
with Jesus Christ. Of course, the prayerful, meditative reading of the Gospel is a paramount means of our getting to
know Christ.

Because Jesus is known by the mind and the heart, our
personal Christology will always involve both. Because this
is so, our relationship has to involve not only reading and
study but also prayer and contemplation. To deepen our personal Christology and to grow in our relationship with him
require a serious commitment of our time and our heart. It
needs to be the principal relationship of our life. An image
of this relationship, fostered by contemplative prayer, can
be found in Mary of Bethany who, it is written, "sat at the
Lord's feet and listened to his teaching" (Lk. 10:39).

Another critical dimension to this relationship is living
in keeping with Christ's teachings. The more we strive to

do this, to see and serve him in others, the deeper will be our true knowledge of him. He himself teaches us this:

> I was hungry and you gave me food, I was thirsty and you gave me drink. I was a stranger and you welcomed me, I was naked and you clothed me, I was sick and you visited me, I was in prison and you came to me. (Mt. 25:35–36)

An obstacle to a proper understanding and relationship to Christ can be one's personal moral life. Jesus himself expresses it starkly in John's Gospel:

> The light came into the world, and men loved darkness rather than light, because their deeds were evil. For every one who does evil hates the light; and does not come to the light lest his deeds should be exposed. (Jn. 3:19–20)

A life of true virtue is essential to develop a proper personal Christology and come to a deeper relationship with Jesus. This does not mean that we are saints. We all remain redeemed sinners engaged in the daily struggle against evil within us and around us. But we cannot hope to truly know Christ while we freely choose to live in a manner that contradicts his teaching.

I used to ask my students to share with me the title that they felt best expressed their personal encounter with Christ. Their responses reflect the wide variety of ways in which each of us relates to Jesus with our personal Christology.

Let me share some of these:

"**Jesus as Carpenter:** Speaks to me in that he lived a human life that can be understood by all. He toiled, he paid taxes, he went to the synagogue on the Sabbath. He ate, bathed, and did every other basic human act aside from sin.

"He gave, therefore, special meaning to all the mundane things of life. He lived as an ordinary man in the backwater of an insignificant region of the world, he truly entered into solidarity with the human situation."

"**Prince of Peace:** In this day and age, it seems that every nation, group, religion, cause, or individual finds it almost impossible to live in peace with other nations, groups, religions, causes, and other individuals. It seems that people find it too hard to be at peace with themselves most of all. This overwhelming need for external and internal peace in the world is why the image of Jesus as 'Prince of Peace' is so powerful to me."

"**Jesus as Good Shepherd:** I can place my hope and trust in him as a sure guide and protector amidst the dangers of the world. I am comforted by our Lord's invitation, 'Come to me, all who labor and are heavy laden, and I will give you rest. Take my yoke upon you and learn from me; for I am gentle and lowly in heart, and you will find rest for your souls' (Mt. 11:28–29)"

"**Jesus as My Lord:** Through my belief in Jesus as Lord, my relationship with him calls me into action. When I made Jesus the Lord of my financial life, I was able to control my spending and start saving and living within my means. When I made Jesus the Lord of my sexuality, I was able to reclaim purity and live in ways that avoided sin. The image of Jesus has been helpful to me in letting the power of Jesus, the Son of God and Son of Mary, into my life and bring me closer to God."

Each of us can probably identify with different aspects of these titles, images, and experiences. In the multifaceted mystery that is Christ, different dimensions may attract us. Jean Vanier speaks of himself as touched by the sheer goodness of Jesus:

> There is no harshness in him. In him resides a deep humility and the innocent love of a child calling, waiting, to give life. Jesus the gentle lover and healer, calls each one of us to fullness and to life disturbing us in our pride, fear, and blockages in order to call forth the light in each of us.[1]

There is a legitimate pluralism in Christology because the mystery of Jesus is like a multifaceted jewel held up to the light that radiates an infinite variety of beauty and light. There are many images of Jesus and, as one author has noted, "The images complement each other, woven together more like a tapestry than ten discrete pictures in a gallery. Jesus is one. He cannot be cut apart and looked at like a limb in a scanner."[2]

Christ has been portrayed in a wide variety of works of art.[3] The frescoes of the Roman catacombs depict him as the

Good Shepherd, while centuries later he is depicted in the golden icons of Byzantium as the majestic Pantocrator.[4] Medieval piety depicted him in realistic crucifixes manifesting both his suffering humanity and his love. In our day the painting of the Christ of Divine Mercy revealed to St. Faustina Kowalska has touched many persons deeply.

This legitimate pluralism underscores one important theological truth: Jesus is absolute mystery. There never was and never will be anyone like him! As John Paul II expressed it: "Who he was is an unfathomable secret." It is for this reason that Jesus could say, " No one knows the Son except the Father" (Mt. 11:27). The Son, however, has revealed himself to us — but our knowledge is always limited and partial and can never hope to fully penetrate or exhaust his mystery

This truth has been well-expressed by a theologian who has devoted his life to this subject:

> Christians do not hold that mere language can be rich enough to express everything about Christ, or at least everything that they wish to express about who he is and what he has done. Much of their tradition of Christological interpretation has come through various styles of life, commitment towards those in need, public worship's symbolic gestures, music, painting, sculpture, architecture, and other nonverbal forms of communication. Christological language has its undoubted point and purpose. But Christian faith has more to express about Jesus as Son of God and Savior of the world than can be contained in words.[5]

In our relationship with Jesus, there will also always be an inevitable distance and also a sense of our unworthiness. We may often feel like Peter — who, after experiencing Jesus' power and holiness exclaimed, "Depart from me, for I am a sinful man, O Lord" (Lk. 5:8). This is a wholesome dimension of any personal Christology. In the presence of God Incarnate we all need to have a humble and contrite heart and gratefully receive his mercy.

The remainder of this book attempts to take the reader beyond his or her personal Christology to deepen and enrich it and, if necessary, correct any inadequacies in it. It does this by exploring how the faith community understood and expressed its experience of the mystery of Christ especially in the Scriptures and in the dogmas of the Church. These are the normative benchmarks for an authentic and complete Christology.

The following list of questions may be helpful in analyzing your personal Christology.

1. What is your favorite image of Jesus?
2. What is your favorite title for Jesus?
3. How do you address him in prayer?
4. What is your favorite Scripture passage about Jesus? Why?
5. When/how did you have your most important /powerful experience of Jesus? Describe it.
6. What aspect of Jesus' person/message do you most wish to transmit to others? Why?
7. What are the chief sources of your personal Christology?
8. What are the chief changes in your Christology over your faith journey thus far?

Endnotes — Chapter 1

[1] Jean Vanier, *Jesus: The Gift of Love* (New York: Crossroads Publishing Co., 1994), p. 11.

[2] Ten images of Jesus are explored in a wonderful book by Rev. Alfred McBride, O. Praem., entitled *Images of Jesus: Ten Invitations to Intimacy* (Cincinnati: St. Anthony Messenger Press and Franciscan Communications, 1992).

[3] See Jaroslov Pelikan, *Jesus through the Centuries* (New Haven, CT: Yale University Press, 1999).

[4] See Christoph Schönborn, *God's Human Face: The Christ Icon* (Ft. Collins, CO: Ignatius Press, 1994).

[5] Gerald O'Collins, S.J., *Christology: A Biblical, Historical and Systematic Study of Jesus* (Oxford: Oxford University Press, 1995), pp. 13-14.

CHAPTER 2

SOURCES AND METHODOLOGY

Although each person has his or her own personal experience and image of Jesus, we must also search for the true face of the authentic Jesus Christ. Our images and approaches need to be deepened and perhaps purified or corrected by a full and complete discovery of the true Lord Jesus.

This journey of prayerful discovery begins with two basic and interrelated issues: What sources will lead us to the truth about Jesus and what method can we follow to ensure a complete and valid Christology? An obvious answer is that our chief source would be Sacred Scripture.

Walter Cardinal Kasper, however, modifies this answer appropriately:

> The New Testament writings exist only because Jesus produced a faith that extended beyond his death and because his first believers collected together, handed on (orally), and finally set down in writing the reports on Jesus. They did this for the needs of their communities, for their liturgy, for

religious instruction (catechesis), and for missionary preaching. The existential location of the writing of the Jesus tradition is the Church. Jesus of
Nazareth is accessible to us only by way of the faith
of the first Christian Churches.[1]

The Scriptures are writings of and by the Church. They
can only be understood properly in the context of the living,
Spirit-filled Church. The Lord Jesus founded a faith community and promised it "the Spirit of truth" who would
"guide you into all truth" (Jn. 16:13). He never urged his
followers to write a Bible!

Christ first commanded the Apostles to preach the
Gospel. In keeping with this command, the Gospel was
handed on in two ways: orally by preaching and later in writing under the inspiration of the Holy Spirit. This living
transmission is called Tradition. The first generation of
Christians did not yet have a written New Testament.

The writing of the Scriptures was a decision made by
the Church, inspired by the Holy Spirit. This decision was
made to facilitate the Church's mission of evangelization.
The Scriptures are therefore Spirit-inspired ecclesial writings and can only be properly received and understood in
the context of the living community of faith that is the
Church, which gave birth to them in the first place.

A Biblical-Ecclesial Methodology

For these reasons, Archbishop Angelo Amato has coined
the term "the biblical-ecclesial methodology" to express the
proper approach to find the true face of Jesus Christ. He thus

brings together the Scripture as a primary source but always as understood in and by the Church (the *ecclesia*).[2]

Amato points out four fundamental elements of such a "biblical-ecclesial" methodology:

1. We begin with the "Story of Jesus": his human history must be constitutive of any correct methodology. His personal journey, including his ministry, teaching, miracles, formation of a community, passion, and death are all foundational to discover the complete portrait of Jesus.

This "story" has always a two-fold aspect: actual historical events that occurred in definite space and time in Palestine 2,000 years ago that were also at the same time salvific interventions of God. Jesus is both a Jewish man of his era and the Christ, the Spirit-filled "Holy One of God" (Mk. 1:24) bringing salvation. The earliest Scripture texts present us with this unified Jesus.

2. There is a basic continuity between the Jesus of history and the Christ of faith. In the Christ Event, faith and history are inextricably united. Those who witnessed the actual words and deeds of Jesus handed them on to us accurately with the faith that was born of their Easter and Pentecost experience.

3. This method, arising from the faith and witness of the primitive Church, presumes and proclaims Jesus as universal and definitive Savior of all who are saved: "There is salvation in no one else, for there is no other name under heaven given among men by which we must be saved" (Acts 4:12).

4. Christology and Soteriology (theology of salvation), therefore, go hand in hand. Christology
answers the question, "Who is Jesus?" Soteriology
answers the question, "What did he do and how
does it affect us?" However, there is an intrinsic
unity between the mystery of the Incarnation of the
Son of God and the mystery of our redemption — as
we shall see in subsequent chapters. For our methodological concern here it is important to simply
underline that we must focus on the salvific relevance for us of Jesus' life in an integral Christology.
Such a Christology demonstrates not only the rec-
onciliation with God Christ effected, but how he
answers the riddle of human existence. In the often
repeated words of *Gaudium et Spes*, the Vatican II
Constitution on the Church in the Modern World,
"Only in the Mystery of the Incarnate Word does
the mystery of man take on light. Christ the Lord
fully reveals man to himself"(#22).

Understanding the source and method of Christology
in this way, we realize that our Christological confession is
more than the fruit of human research or academic scriptural exegesis. It is a divine illumination! "No one can say
'Jesus is Lord' except by the Holy Spirit" (1 Cor. 12:3). From
the start of our study of the person of Christ it is critical to
keep this basic truth in mind.

Though we are not dispensed from the rational investi-
gation, justification, and defense of our faith, a humble heart
is always required to draw us into the full Christian mystery
that always exceeds human reason. Indeed, human reason

staggers before the wonder of God's self-emptying manifested in the incarnation of God's Eternal Son as Jesus of Nazareth. Any theological methodology must be fully illumined by the working in us of the Holy Spirit:

> The Spirit searches everything, even the depths of God. For what person knows a man's thoughts except the Spirit of the man which is in him? So also no one comprehends the thoughts of God except the Spirit of God. Now we have received not the spirit of the world, but the Spirit which is from God, that we might understand the gifts bestowed on us by God. And we impart this in words not taught by human wisdom but taught by the Spirit, interpreting spiritual truths to those who possess the Spirit. The unspiritual man does not receive the gifts of the Spirit of God, for they are folly to him, and he is not able to understand them because they are spiritually discerned. (1 Cor. 2:10–14)

The Scriptures as Sources

The Scriptures, inspired by the Holy Spirit and compiled by the Church, are the primary source of our knowledge about the truth of Christ. They give us a historically reliable foundation for our faith. Luke expresses well the intention of the Gospel writers: "It seemed good to me also, having followed all things closely for some time past, to write an orderly account for you" (Lk. 1:3).

Each of the four Evangelists adapted the oral traditions he received as he wrote his Gospel with the situation and needs of a particular Church in mind. Yet, there is a remarkable convergence in these different Gospel traditions that were put in writing at different times and places. The reader will want to become acquainted with the various Gospel commentaries that help one to see the special characteristics of each Gospel.

The open-minded and unbiased reader of the Gospel will quickly share "the Church's conviction that the four Gospels together, in their relative contradictions and essential complementarity, provide the full, authentic portrait of Jesus and the full authentic depositary of his teachings."[3] From these Gospel sources our faith has a sufficient and secure historical foundation.

In recent centuries, however, some have questioned this reality. The so-called Enlightenment, an intellectual movement begun in the seventeenth century, introduced a critical and negative spirit into the interpretation of the Scriptures, and this infected many Protestant and even Catholic Scripture scholars.

Enlightenment scholars started with an anti-dogmatic, anti-faith bias that rejected the early Church's understanding of Jesus and denied *a priori* the possibility of an Incarnation, miracles, the Resurrection. Starting with this prejudice, they sought to liberate a "Jesus of History" from the "Christ of faith." They created a false dichotomy that seventeen centuries of Christianity had never known.

New methods of literary and historical criticism combined with rationalist presuppositions hostile to faith brought a spirit of skepticism with regard to the so-called historicity of the Scriptures. In the hand of these exegetes, the Scriptures become divorced from the ecclesial matrix that had produced them and were subjected to purely modern secular criteria of historical authenticity.

This approach resulted in the so-called "Quest for the Historical Jesus," which was launched by Hermann Reimarus at the end of the eighteenth century and continued till the middle of the twentieth century, when the "New Quest for the Historical Jesus" was sparked by Ernst Käsemann in 1953. The "New Quest" rejected the radical approach of Reimarus and others and insisted on the presence of much authentic historical material in the Gospels. Still, even these scholars did not accept adequately the ecclesial context of the Spirit-inspired Scriptures.

An extreme example of this flawed approach to the use of Scriptures is the so-called Jesus Seminar, which claims to go behind the writings to make judgments on the historical reality of Jesus' actual words and deeds discarding much of the Gospel text as "unhistorical."[4]

Responding to what he calls this "non-scholarly liberalism," the American Scripture scholar, Fr. Raymond Brown, S.S., asserts:

> It is far safer to work with the self-understanding of the New Testament writers who thought that they were vocalizing and appreciating a reality that was already there. . . . [Yet there was also] a development during the first century that involves a growing Christian understanding about the identity of Jesus, not the creation *ex-nihilo* of a new identity.[5]

It needs to be said that the tools of modern historical criticism have had many positive results in our understanding of the development of the Scriptures. They highlight the three basic phases of development of the Gospel texts:

1. The actual events in which Jesus was involved and his words
2. The oral traditions that passed them on for decades
3. The editing of these traditions into the four Gospels

In the hands of faithful scholars, the use of these tools has enhanced our knowledge of the development of the Gospel text and the history of Jesus.[6]

In addition to the Gospels, the rest of the New Testament writings also reflect the early Church's understanding of the mystery of Christ. Paul's Epistles, written before the composition of the Gospels, are an important source of our Christological faith and show the growing understanding of the meaning of the Christ Event. We shall follow these developments in subsequent chapters.

Other Sources

In addition to the Scriptures, there are many other sources for developing a full Christology. There are a few references in pagan writings to Christ and his followers. There are the rich reflections of the early Fathers of the Church such as St. Ignatius of Antioch.

Ignatius, for example, expresses in concise form the faith of the earliest Church when he writes:

There is one physician, who is both flesh and spirit, born and not born, who is God in man, true life in death, both from Mary and from God, first able to suffer and then unable to suffer, Jesus Christ, Our Lord. (*Letter to Ephesians*, 7, 2)

A large number of the early Fathers of the Church have rich insights into the mystery of Christ and are important sources of our understanding of Jesus. We shall treat them in subsequent chapters.

Eventually the Church found it necessary in Ecumenical Councils to express in clear dogmatic formulas its faith convictions about the mystery of Christ. These definitions are important sources for a full Christology and these also will be explored in later sections of this book.

From the beginning, the Sacred Liturgy, through its hymns and prayers, has been a living source for our Christology. Some of these earliest prayers, such as Maranatha ("Our Lord, come!"), found their way into the Scriptures (1 Cor. 16:22). Another example is the great Christological hymn of Philippians (Phil. 2:6–11). This tradition of prayer to Christ continued and developed in the Church, providing another source for Christology.

Therefore, in addition to the principal source, which is the New Testament, there are many other sources from which a rich Christology can be developed. We need in turn to examine all of these sources to develop a complete picture of Christ, and we shall attempt to do so in subsequent chapters.

But before doing so, let us end this section on sources with the beautiful words of Archbishop Amato:

Jesus himself is the true treatise on Christology. When he opens his arms on the cross and his heart is pierced, the real book was opened and shown to all. It is sufficient to contemplate the Risen Crucified One to understand the Mystery. Only he, the immolated Lamb, all-powerful and all-knowing, can open the book and break its seven seals. (cf. Rev. 5:2–7). It is a book written on his flesh and poured out from his heart.[7]

Methodological Distinctions

In further considering a Christological methodology that will deepen our understanding of the mystery of Jesus, some distinctions can be helpful. A classical distinction is that between an ascending Christology (from below) and a descending Christology (from above). This is a question of the starting point. An ascending Christology starts from historical Jesus of Nazareth and moves from that to his divine origin and nature. A descending Christology starts from the pre-existent Eternal Son and Word and then moves to his historical Incarnation.

Fr. Karl Rahner, in a classic article on this methodological distinction[8] notes that ascending Christology focuses "first on the man, Jesus of Nazareth, and on him in his fully human reality, in his death, in his absolute powerlessness. The eye of faith rests upon this man Jesus." He further explains that descending Christology, in contrast, begins with "the pre-existence of the Logos," his divinity, and then shows how this "pre-existent Logos also achieves a visibly historical dimension."

In modern times, when the issue of history is so central and when there is a great focus on the human person, ascending Christology may be a preferred approach, and this book basically takes that approach. Nonetheless, the two approaches are really complementary and can never be totally separated: Jesus is one person, both human and divine at the same time.

Overemphasizing one approach over another can create methodological problems for Christology. Too exclusive a use of a descending Christology runs the risk of minimizing the true and real humanity of Jesus, whereas too exclusive a use of an ascending Christology runs the risk of minimizing Jesus' true divinity.

In the New Testament itself we find both approaches. The Synoptic Gospels emphasize an ascending Christology in which the historical Jesus of Nazareth gradually reveals his messiahship and divine sonship. John's Gospel, rather, begins with a descending Christology, "The Word became flesh and dwelt among us" (Jn. 1:14).

Another set of names for this same methodological distinction is "Christology from below" (ascending) and "Christology from above" (descending). An authentic and balanced Christology needs to harmonize both approaches.

Another related helpful methodological distinction is that between a functional Christology and an ontological Christology. Functional Christology focuses on what the historical Jesus taught and did for us. Ontological Christology focuses on his true essence and being as a divine person who became man. Again, these two dimensions are complementary not contradictory.

The early Christians were neither philosophers nor theologians, and so the Christology reflected in much of the New Testament is primarily functional rather than ontological. Their concern was the great saving deed that God had done in and through Jesus. One looks in vain for the kind of sophisticated philosophical clarity that came with the definitions of the Church Councils of the fourth and fifth centuries. Yet behind this functional Christology was a clear understanding of that divine Sonship that made possible the salvation Jesus effected.

Some modern Protestant scholars have propagated an almost totally functional approach to Christology (e.g., R. Bultmann).

> It is doubtful that any can propose a purely functional Christology, one that attends only to Christ's saving activity on our behalf and refuses to raise any ontological questions whatever about who and what he is in himself. According to a classical axiom, "action follows being" (*agere sequitur esse*). To reflect on the activity of Christ, while denying all knowledge of his being, would be to attempt the impossible.[9]

These reflections and clarifications on sources and methods make it possible for us now to turn more intensely to an examination of the Scriptural sources themselves in our efforts to discover the true face of Jesus of Nazareth.

Endnotes — Chapter 2

[1] Walter Kasper, *Jesus the Christ* (New York: Paulist Press, 1976), p. 26.

[2] Angelo Amato, *Gesù il Signore* (Bologna: Edizioni Dehoniane, 2003), pp. 72-86.

[3] Roch Kereszty, *Jesus Christ: Fundamentals of Christology* (New York: Alba House, 2002), p. 4.

[4] For a critical examination of these efforts, see L.T. Johnson, *The Real Jesus* (San Francisco: Harper Co., 1999).

[5] Raymond Brown, *An Introduction to the New Testament Christology* (New York: Paulist Press 1994), p. 109.

[6] See John Meier's monumental work, *A Marginal Jew* (New York: Doubleday; 3 Volumes, 1991, 1994, 2001).

[7] Karl Rahner, "The Two Basic Types of Christology," *Theological Investigations* (New York: Crossroads, 1983), Vol. 13, p. 213-223.

[8] For a sophisticated treatment of this transition, see Bernard Lonergan, *The Way to Nicea* (Philadelphia: Westminster Press, 1976).

[9] Gerald O' Collins, *Christology: A Biblical, Historical and Systematic Study of Jesus Christ* (Oxford: Oxford University Press, 1995), p. 20.

CHAPTER 3

OLD TESTAMENT PREPARATION

God has a harmonious and unified plan for the human family, which results in what is called "salvation history." This history begins with creation and will culminate with the Parousia — the glorious return and triumph of Our Lord Jesus Christ. In between, God is constantly calling his people to friendship with himself.

God's plan has gradually unfolded over centuries and millennia. We could say that he adapts himself to the capacity of his creatures, and so only gradually reveals the full truth of his saving love and our full dignity and destiny. There is, therefore, a strong continuity between the revelation that began in the Old Testament and reached a climax in the New Testament.

The very word testament, which signifies covenant, suggests this continuity. God has made one covenant with the human family, which has unfolded gradually, beginning especially with Abraham, solemnly celebrated by Moses (see Exodus 24), and reaching its highest realization when Jesus declared, "This chalice is the new covenant in my blood" (1 Cor. 11:25). It is now for all people.

This continuous "history of salvation" is proclaimed in
the Letter to the Hebrews:

> In many and various ways God spoke of old to our
> fathers by the prophets; but in these last days he has
> spoken to us by a Son, whom he appointed the heir
> of all things, through whom he also created the ages.
> (Heb. 1:1–2)

One contemporary writer has put it well:

> God's descent into history in the person of Christ
> was not a solitary, isolated event: it stood in a long
> train of earlier appearances of God to the people of
> Israel. Without this history the significance of
> Christ's coming was hidden. . . . The God who
> appeared in Christ was the Lord who appeared to
> Abraham, Isaac, and Jacob, to Sarah, and Rebecca
> and Rachel, to kings and prophets and sages of old.
> The Christian Gospel does not appear in a vacuum,
> it is of a piece with the revelation of God to Israel.[1]

The Second Vatican Council, in its Constitution on
Divine Revelation, *Dei Verbum*, emphasizes this unified, harmonious, divine plan. After noting the call of Abraham, the
mission of Moses, and the prophets, it declares that God
taught Israel

> to acknowledge Himself as the one living and true
> God, provident father and just judge, and to wait

for the Savior promised by Him, and in this manner prepared the way for the Gospel. (*Dei Verbum*, 3)

For these reasons Fr. Gerald O'Collins has rightly said: "A Christology that ignores or plays down the Old Testament can only be radically deficient. . . . The Old Testament is essential for grasping the New Testament Christological message."[2]

Four Contributions of the Old Testament

We can highlight four ways in which the Old Testament Scriptures lay the foundation for New Testament Christological faith.

1. Dynamism of Salvation

The Old Testament proclaims what Fr. Jean Galot calls "a dynamism of salvation."[3] The people of Israel experienced God as Savior in a way that was unique among the religions of ancient times. They sensed themselves objects of God's special care and believed that he had personally intervened to rescue them from their situation of slavery and oppression in Egypt. This experience and these ideas made Israel ready for the later concept of a Messianic, anointed deliverer.

Related to this was a new conception of God — a God who was near his people, cared about his people, and intervened in history to save them.

This new vision of God was expressed in the words Yahweh addressed to Moses:

> I have seen the affliction of my people who are in
> Egypt, and have heard their cry because of their
> taskmasters; I know their sufferings, and I have
> come down to deliver them out of the hand of the
> Egyptians and to bring them up out of that land to
> a good and broad land. (Ex. 3:7–8)

From Abraham through the Prophets, it is made clear
that God is a faithful God who will not abandon his people.
Even their constant unfaithfulness to the covenant does not
deter God's saving purpose. He allows them to be purified by
the destruction of Jerusalem and the exile, but he never
abandons them.

> I will re-establish my covenant with you, and you
> shall know that I am the LORD, that you may
> remember and be confounded, and never open your
> mouth again because of your shame, when I forgive
> you for all that you have done, says the Lord GOD.
> (Ezek. 16:62–63)

Israel came to know God as a Savior God who was faithful and always sought new ways to bring his people to conversion and renewal. These convictions prepared the way
for Jesus to appear and be recognized precisely as "Savior" or
anointed Deliverer.

2. Dynamism of Incarnation

Fr. Galot also sees growing throughout the Old Testament
what he calls "a dynamism of Incarnation." God's closeness to
his people takes on tangible forms. Throughout the Old Tes-

tament God is constantly drawing closer to his people. He travels with them in the pillar of fire and in the cloud. He prescribes concrete, tangible signs of his closeness and his presence to them such as the Tent of Meeting:

> Now Moses used to take the tent and pitch it out-side the camp, far off from the camp; and he called it the tent of meeting. And every one who sought the LORD would go out to the tent of meeting, which was outside the camp. Whenever Moses went out to the tent, all the people rose up, and every man stood at his tent door, and looked after Moses, until he had gone into the tent. When Moses entered the tent, the pillar of cloud would descend and stand at the door of the tent, and the LORD would speak with Moses. (Ex. 33:7–9)

This presence of God to his people — known as the Shekinah — allowed them to recognize the divine presence in their midst. The Holy of Holies in the Jerusalem temple became a special sign of his presence.

Through all of this, the way is being prepared in the hearts of the Chosen People for God to finally manifest him-self in the most tangible form imaginable as "Emmanuel — God With Us," God in flesh.

3. Concept of Mediation

The Old Testament already shows God making use of different forms of human mediation and instrumentality to achieve his saving purposes for his people.

The Pontifical Biblical Commission, in its document on Scripture and Christology, highlights this special contribution of the Old Testament to Christology.[4] It notes the roles of kings, priests, and prophets as mediators of salvation in the Old Testament.

Israel's kings in the Old Testament were not just political rulers — they were anointed by God to be agents of his saving purpose for his people. Priests were guardians and interpreters of God's law and offered sacrifices of expiation for the people. Prophets spoke in God's name calling the people to conversion, a new way of life and to faithfulness to the Covenant.

Despite the people's lack of fidelity, God remained faithful, and, in the later stages of Old Testament salvation history, the hope of a new and more effective mediator arose, through whose activity God's Kingdom would be effectively inaugurated once and for all.

The prophets spoke often about this future mediator who would rescue the people and be the agent of salvation. Even though it seemed all hope had been lost and the dynasty of David was reduced to a mere stump, Isaiah was confident enough in God to utter his famous Messianic oracle:

There shall come forth a shoot from the stump of Jesse, and a branch shall grow out of his roots. And the Spirit of the LORD shall rest upon him, and the spirit of wisdom and understanding, the spirit of counsel and might, the spirit of knowledge and the fear of the LORD. And his delight shall be in the fear of the LORD.

He shall not judge by what his eyes see, or decide by what his ears hear; but with righteousness he shall judge the poor, and decide with equity for the meek of the earth; and he shall strike the earth with the rod of his mouth, and with the breath of his lips he shall slay the wicked. Righteousness shall be the belt of his waist, and faithfulness the belt of his loins.

The wolf shall dwell with the lamb, and the leopard shall lie down with the kid, and the calf and the lion and the fatling together, and a little child shall lead them. The cow and the bear shall feed; their young shall lie down together; and the lion shall eat straw like the ox. The suckling child shall play over the hole of the asp, and the weaned child shall put his hand on the adder's den. They shall not hurt or destroy in all my holy mountain; for the earth shall be full of the knowledge of the LORD as the waters cover the sea. In that day the root of Jesse shall stand as an ensign to the peoples; him shall the nations seek, and his dwellings shall be glorious. (Is. 11:1–10)

The Pontifical Biblical Commission document highlights three of the mediating roles that were fulfilled completely in Christ:

a) **The King-Messiah** — would be the perfect, ideal king who would definitively establish God's peace and justice; he would be the true descendant of King

David to whom God promised universal sovereignty
(see 2 Sam. 7).

b) **The Servant of the Lord** — highlighted especially
in Isaiah, chapters 52–53, who would bear the
weight of the people's sins and reconcile them to
the Lord.

c) **The Mysterious Son of Man of Daniel** — in
Daniel, chapter 7 — to whom would be given power
over all peoples and a share in God's sovereignty.

4. Theological Vocabulary

The Old Testament further provided some of the most
important concepts and terms that early Christians later
used to express their understanding of Christ's identity and
mystery. As Fr. Gerald O'Collins puts it, the early Christian
"quarried" in the Old Testament text to find ideas and language to express their faith in Christ.

We shall examine this process more thoroughly when
we investigate the development of Christology in the early
Church. Let us simply note now that the Old Testament
concept of Wisdom — a pre-existing "being" that appears to
share God's creative work — was helpful to early Christians
in their understanding of the pre-existent functions of the
eternal Son.

This concept can be found in Proverbs 8:22–30, Wisdom
8:4–6 and 9:9–10, and Sirach 1:4–9. It is for the eyes of Christian faith a foreshadowing of the mystery of the Trinity:

The LORD created me at the beginning of his work,
the first of his acts of old. Ages ago I was set up, at
the first, before the beginning of the earth. When he

established the heavens, I was there, when he drew
a circle on the face of the deep, when he made firm
the skies above, when he established the fountains
of the deep . . . when he marked out the foundations
of the earth, then I was beside him, like a master
workman. (Prov. 8:22, 27–30)

All we have just noted emphasizes the importance of an
understanding of and respect for the Old Testament, the
Jewish Scriptures. They are essential for our understanding
of Jesus. He appears in the stream of Jewish religious thought
and faith. While there is a startling novelty about him, there
is also continuity with the religion of Israel. His mission is a
continuation and a fulfillment of God's saving work begun
with his chosen people.

Pope Pius XI said, "We are all spiritually Semites." This
slogan reflects the profound insight of Paul the Apostle
about the inextricable relationship between Judaism and
Christianity (elaborated in Romans 9–11). This relationship continues and the Jews participate in God's covenant
perhaps in ways we cannot fully comprehend or express. As
Paul reminds us, "The gifts and the call of God are irrevoca-
ble" (Rom. 11:29).

In our present context, therefore, we need to acknowl-
edge in concluding this section how truly New Testament
Christology is dependent upon its Old Testament foundations and how this fact emphasizes the single saving plan
of God.

Endnotes — Chapter 3

[1] Robert Wilken, *The Spirit of Early Christian Thought* (New Haven, CT: Yale University Press, 2003), p. 16.

[2] Gerald O'Collins, *Christology: A Biblical, Historical and Systematic Study of Jesus* (Oxford: Oxford University Press, 1995), p. 23.

[3] Jean Galot, *The Eternal Son* (Huntington, IN: Our Sunday Visitor Press, 1978).

[4] See the complete text with commentary in Joseph Fitzmyer, *Scripture and Christology* (New York: Paulist Press, 1986).

CHAPTER 4

THE HISTORICAL JESUS: THE MYSTERY AND THE MESSAGE

Jesus appears on the public stage in about his thirtieth year. It is very significant that his first public gesture is an act of humility and profound solidarity with sinful humanity:

> Then Jesus came from Galilee to the Jordan to John, to be baptized by him. John would have prevented him, saying, "I need to be baptized by you, and do you come to me?" But Jesus answered him, "Let it be so now; for thus it is fitting for us to fulfil all righteousness." (Mt. 3:13–15)

Jesus does not make any claim to special privilege or demand recognition — he gets in line with sinners — he has come to be one with us.

From the start, however, Jesus seems to exert a powerful attraction. He comes from obscure Nazareth, apparently a carpenter's son, with no formal schooling and credentials. Yet, it appears to be the power and mystery of his very person that somehow seems to draw people strongly from the start.

An early recollection of this is contained in John's Gospel:

> The next day again John was standing with two of his disciples; and he looked at Jesus as he walked, and said, "Behold, the Lamb of God!" The two disciples heard him say this, and they followed Jesus. Jesus turned, and saw them following, and said to them, "What do you seek?" And they said to him, "Rabbi" (which means Teacher), "where are you staying?" He said to them, "Come and see." They came and saw where he was staying; and they stayed with him that day, for it was about the tenth hour. One of the two who heard John speak, and followed him, was Andrew, Simon Peter's brother. He first found his brother Simon, and said to him, "We have found the Messiah" (which means Christ). (Jn. 1:35–41)

The number of disciples grew as Jesus began to speak in the synagogues and hills of his native Galilee, the northern part of Palestine.

The essential departure point for Christology is this earthly and historical figure of Jesus of Nazareth who is often referred to as the "pre-paschal Jesus" — Jesus before his Passion and Resurrection. It is with him that the early Church began its preaching and catechesis. Peter, in one of his earliest catecheses, said:

> You know the word which he sent to the sons of Israel, preaching good news of peace by Jesus Christ

(he is the Lord of all), the word which was proclaimed throughout all Judea, beginning from
Galilee after the baptism which John preached: how
God anointed Jesus of Nazareth with the Holy Spirit
and with power; how he went about doing good and
healing all that were oppressed by the devil, for God
was with him. (Acts 10:36–38)

From this perspective, it is clear that we are dealing here
with an ascending and functional Christology. This
approach to Jesus reminds us of the important truth that
Christianity is not primarily a philosophy or an ideology. It
is rather totally based on an event, the Christ Event. It is a
proclamation about a person and things that happened at a
specific time and place and that were the means of God's
saving intervention in history. Theology does not create
these events — rather it seeks to understand and explain
them. It is totally subordinate to the mystery embodied in
the events.

It was the early disciples' actual experience of this historical Christ Event: his pre-paschal ministry of preaching,
miracles, and gathering of community; and his passion,
death, and resurrection that led to the formation of the
Church and its desire to formulate a remembrance of these
events that became the Scriptures and the Creeds. Both are
dependent on the primary experience of the earliest followers of Jesus. As St. John expresses it:

That which was from the beginning, which we
have heard, which we have seen with our eyes,
which we have looked upon and touched with our

hands, concerning the word of life — the life was made manifest, and we saw it, and testify to it, and proclaim to you the eternal life which was with the Father and was made manifest to us — that which we have seen and heard we proclaim also to you, so that you may have fellowship with us; and our fellowship is with the Father and with his Son Jesus Christ. (1 Jn. 1:1–3)

Background

It is important to recognize that Jesus was immersed in a particular specific historical and cultural setting. Certainly this is one of the purposes of the lengthy genealogy of Jesus with which Matthew begins his Gospel. He makes a point of showing Jesus' human connection with a line of ancestors who in some cases were less than admirable (Mt. 1:1–17). His point is that Jesus came in the stream of Jewish history, a descendant of David.

In 63 B.C., the Roman occupation of Palestine began, and the Jewish King Herod ruled as a puppet of the Romans. Sometimes Roman troops marched from Damascus in Syria to Jerusalem and passed along the road near Nazareth. Can we not imagine the young Jesus and his friends going out to see them pass as their golden breastplates gleamed in the sun? He was aware of the resentment his fellow Jews felt toward these conquerors.

Surrounded by this alien hostile culture, Jews reacted in various ways. There was a significant amount of pluralism among the Jews of Jesus' time. To be sure, all shared a basic belief in monotheism (one God), the special choice of Israel by God, the Covenant, and the Law's importance. Still, there was considerable diversity.

There were in Jesus' time four basic groups:

The **Pharisees** emphasized strict faithfulness to the Law as the means to preserve Jewish identity. They developed elaborate and detailed rules to enforce this approach to their faith. Their place of influence was primarily the local synagogue, and they had the respect of the ordinary people for their obvious piety and fidelity. They believed in the resurrection of the dead and looked for the coming of the Messiah.

The **Sadducees** represented the priestly families, and their chief focus was on Temple worship. They collaborated with the Roman authorities. Their concerns were focused on the temple ritual observance. They were anxious not to antagonize the Roman rulers so that they could continue their religious practices. They were led by the High Priest. They rejected beliefs such as the resurrection of the body.

The **Essenes** sought to withdraw from the political world and live a life of austerity and purity while they awaited a direct intervention from God to overthrow the Romans and establish his Kingdom. The Dead Sea Scrolls told us about this group.

The **Zealots** were smaller groups who were not content to await God's intervention but took matters in their own hands. They were in the modern sense guerilla warriors or terrorists who would perform rebellious acts to disrupt Roman rule.

Jesus interacted with these various groups throughout his ministry and frequently was in conflict with them for different reasons. He was not associated with any of them and so in a certain sense was on the fringe of Jewish society. For this reason, Scripture scholar Msgr. John Meier calls him "a marginal Jew."

In a more positive way, we could say that Jesus' approach was a prophetic one, a visionary one that looked beyond the present passing political situation to God's purpose and Kingdom. He was a man standing at the edge of his society pointing beyond to something greater and more lasting — the ultimate Kingdom of God — of which he was the herald.

Msgr. Meier's monumental work tells us that Jesus' public ministry began somewhere between A.D. 26 and 29 and went till somewhere between A.D. 28 and 33. He was probably in his early to mid-thirties at the beginning of his public ministry.[2]

His name, Yeshua, was unremarkable — many Jewish children would have been so named. It was the name of the great general, Joshua, who succeeded Moses as leader of the people. As Msgr. Meier points out: "So current was the name Jesus that some descriptive phrase like "of Nazareth" or "the Christ (Messiah)" had to be added to distinguish him from many other bearers of that name" (A Marginal Jew, Vol. 1, p. 206).

The Son

In evaluating any person, we always want to know, "What was the driving force of his life? What was his primary motivation? His inspiration?" This is also critical to evaluating the human, historical Jesus of Nazareth.

From the start and throughout his ministry, it is clear that his lodestar was God whom he knew and addressed in a unique and intimate way as "Abba, Father" (Mk. 14:36). His profound filial consciousness was clearly the foundation of his life and ministry. This was what was remarkable about Jesus of Nazareth and singled him out. This is powerfully expressed in his prayer to the Father:

> I thank you, Father, Lord of heaven and earth, that you have hidden these things from the wise and understanding and revealed them to infants. . . . All things have been delivered to me by my Father; and no one knows the Father except the Son and any one to whom the Son chooses to reveal him. (Mt. 11:25, 27)

We do not have full access to the human consciousness and interior knowledge of Jesus, but it appears that his baptism may have been the occasion of a stronger and deeper awareness of his filial condition:

> In those days Jesus came from Nazareth of Galilee and was baptized by John in the Jordan. And when he came up out of the water, immediately he saw the heavens opened and the Spirit descending upon him like a dove; and a voice came from heaven, "You are my beloved Son; with you I am well pleased." (Mk. 1:9–11)

Jesus knew and spoke of God the Father as no one ever had, and he did so with confidence and simplicity. An intimate, habitual awareness of the Father was connatural to him. He addressed him by the familiar term of "Abba" (Daddy), which was not done by his fellow Jews.

In the major decisions of his life Jesus goes to the mountains to pray to immerse himself in the Father's will. When others wish to exploit him as a miracle worker, we read:

> And in the morning, a great while before day, he rose and went out to a lonely place, and there he prayed. And Simon and those who were with him followed him, and they found him and said to him, "Every one is searching for you." And he said to them, "Let us go on to the next towns, that I may preach there also, for that is why I came out." And he went throughout all Galilee, preaching in their synagogues and casting out demons. (Mk. 1:35–39)

At the end of his ministry, he prays again, "Abba, Father, all things are possible to you; remove this chalice from me; yet not what I will, but what you will" (Mk. 14:36). John captures well Jesus' inner spirit when he has him say, "I do as the Father has commanded me, so that the world may know that I love the Father" (Jn. 14:31).

From this innate familiarity with the Father flows Jesus' teaching. Because he knows deeply the goodness and faithfulness of the Father, he can urge followers toward total trust in the Father:

> Look at the birds of the air: they neither sow nor reap nor gather into barns, and yet your heavenly Father feeds them. Are you not of more value than they? And which of you by being anxious can add one cubit to his span of life? And why are you anxious about clothing? Consider the lilies of the field,

how they grow; they neither toil nor spin; yet I tell
you, even Solomon in all his glory was not clothed
like one of these. But if God so clothes the grass of
the field, which today is alive and tomorrow is
thrown into the oven, will he not much more clothe
you, O you of little faith? Therefore do not be anxious, saying, "What shall we eat?" or "What shall we
drink?" or "What shall we wear?" For the Gentiles
seek all these things; and your heavenly father
knows that you need them all. But seek first his
kingdom and his righteousness, and all these things
shall be yours as well. (Mt. 6:26–33)

Fr. Karl Rahner, S.J., summarizes well the impact Jesus'
filial consciousness had on those who heard him:

At last there was someone in our midst, someone
who knew something . . . someone who gave a name
to the incomprehensible puzzle behind all things
— he called it his "Father" — and did so with neither incredible naivete nor with tasteless presump-
tion. He was unassumingly wise and good. He
invited us, too, to whisper into the darkness, "Our
Father." At last we were able to know and imagine
something about God besides the abstraction of
philosophers. At last, there was someone who knew
something (about the great mystery) and yet did
not have to speak with clever eloquence but with
beautiful simplicity.[3]

The Message

The Scriptures tells us Jesus spent the nearly three years of his public ministry as an itinerant preacher and teacher on the hillsides and plains of Galilee — wherever he could gather a crowd, he taught and preached. Matthew's Gospel especially is a compendium of the teaching of Jesus. Most probably, "Rabbi" or "Teacher" was the title he most often received. In fact, he is addressed this way 41 times in the Gospels.

His teaching had a strong eschatological dimension. This means that he was announcing the breaking into human history of God's reign; that the promise and hopes of Jewish faith were now being realized and fulfilled in him and in his ministry:

> Jesus came into Galilee, preaching the gospel of God, and saying, "The time is fulfilled, and the kingdom of God is at hand; repent, and believe in the gospel." (Mk. 1:14–15)

A characteristic of his teaching style was the confidence and authority with which he spoke. He knew God and spoke about him in a simple yet powerful way. He spoke of him as the Provident Father (cf. Mt. 6:25–34) as the Merciful and Forgiving Father (cf. Lk. 15:11–32).

He used parables, examples from nature and daily life, as a teaching device to convey his message in a way that could appeal to the imagination and the heart, not just to the mind or intellect. The reaction to his teaching is frequently noted in the Gospels: "They questioned among themselves, saying, 'What is this? A new teaching! With authority he commands even the unclean spirits and they obey him'" (Mk. 1:27).

His teaching invited his hearers to a personal familiarity and an intimacy with God not common among Jews at that time and in contrast to the legalistic religion of the Pharisees. Significantly, it was sinners and outcasts who were drawn to him, and to them he gave a call to conversion and a message of hope: "I tell you, there will be more joy in heaven over one sinner who repents than over ninety-nine righteous persons who need no repentance" (Lk. 15:7).

A unifying theme of Jesus preaching and teaching was the Kingdom of God. This expression, rare in first century Judaism, is found often on the lips of Jesus: 25 times in Matthew, 13 times in Mark, 6 times in Luke. As Msgr. John Meier affirms, "These frequent occurrences faithfully reflect Jesus' own usage and emphasis.... The Kingdom of God was a major component of Jesus' message."[4]

As one Scripture scholar says, Jesus' phrase, the "Kingdom of God," is a "tensive symbol" — it has a rich variety of meanings, all meant to conjure up the notion of God ruling dynamically over his people. It emphasizes what God can and will do and calls people to be open and responsive.

Jesus is the herald and indeed the personification of this Kingdom: "If it is by the Spirit of God that I cast out demons, then the kingdom of God has come upon you" (Mt. 12:28).

Jesus' ethical and moral teaching is related to his proclamation of the coming of the Kingdom. Because the Kingdom takes priority over earthly values, he proclaims in the Sermon on the Mount a whole new set of "Kingdom values":

"Blessed are the poor in spirit, for theirs is the king-dom of heaven. Blessed are those who mourn, for they shall be comforted. Blessed are the meek, for they shall inherit the earth. Blessed are those who hunger and thirst for righteousness, for they shall be satisfied. Blessed are the merciful, for they shall obtain mercy. Blessed are the pure in heart, for they shall see God. Blessed are the peacemakers, for they shall be called the sons of God. Blessed are those who are persecuted for righteousness' sake, for theirs is the kingdom of heaven. Blessed are you when men revile you and persecute you and utter all kinds of evil against you falsely on my account. Rejoice and be glad, for your reward is great in heaven, for so men persecuted the prophets who were before you. (Mt. 5:3–12)

Jesus' teaching on the Kingdom underlines an impor-tant theological truth: in the biblical view, man by himself is incapable of producing the full harmony, peace, justice, and freedom the Kingdom represents. The Scriptures do not look for a "better world" in the humanistic sense if people could just "pull themselves together and try harder." The Scriptures speak of a "new heaven" and a "new earth" that God will create. Jesus is announcing that in him this process has started! This is the Kingdom of God that Jesus preaches.

Related to this central theme is a distinction in Jesus' teaching about the Kingdom between an "already-realized," imminent phase and a "not yet," eschatological stage to still be awaited and expected. Jesus urged his followers to pray,

"Thy Kingdom come." While the kingdom was being introduced in his person and deeds, he taught that the final realization of the kingdom was connected to the triumphant
coming of the Son of Man at the end of history. Many of
Jesus' parables deal with this double dimension of the Kingdom: the parables of the mustard seed (Mt. 13:31), yeast
(Mt. 13:33), and the wheat and the weeds (Mt. 13:24–30).
What begins now in a modest way will come to a glorious
realization.

Jesus' proclamation of the Kingdom did not neatly fit
with much of popular Jewish expectation. Significantly, he
never spoke of the Kingdom of David. As Fr. Raymond
Brown notes:

> Jesus proclaimed that the kingdom was at hand, but
> his notion of kingdom did not fit the anticipation in
> many ways. He spoke of the kingdom (kingship) of
> God, not of David. The kingship that he heralded
> rules over both individual lives and the whole of
> God's people Israel (without any suggestion of geo-
> graphical boundaries). While it touches people on
> earth, it is a kingdom of the last times and, at least
> implicitly, affects all creation. No earthly foreign
> conquerors are fought, for the enemy who resists it
> and must be vanquished is Satan or the devil.[5]

Naturally people wondered when and how this final triumph of the Kingdom would occur. In response, Jesus makes
a strong assertion:

But of that day or that hour no one knows, not even
the angels in heaven, nor the Son, but only the
Father. Take heed, watch and pray; for you do not
know when the time will come. (Mk. 13:32–33)

The Miracles

One of the best attested dimensions of Jesus' pre-paschal
ministry were the many miracles that he worked. The Scriptures refer to "miracles" less in the sense of wonder works
but more so as "acts of power" (Synoptics) or "signs" (John).
The reason for this was that the miracles were means by
which the imminent dimension of the Kingdom in Jesus' life
was manifested. Through them, he was already destroying
the power of Satan that manifested itself in illness and
death. He was bringing God's salvation to the world and to
individuals.[6]

In his first Pentecost season and catechesis, Peter underlined this aspect of the ministry of the historical pre-paschal
Jesus:

Men of Israel, hear these words: Jesus of Nazareth, a
man attested to you by God with mighty works and
wonders and signs which God did through him in
your midst, as you yourselves know. (Acts 2:22)

Jesus' miracles were intended to call attention to his
message of the Kingdom and elicit faith and hope in God
who was at work in and through him. The need for such a
strategy has been well expressed by one of the greatest of the
Fathers of the Church, St Leo the Great:

Because human ignorance is slow to believe what it does not see and equally slow to hope for what it does not know — those who were to be instructed in the divine teaching had first to be aroused by bodily benefits and visible miracles — so that — once they had experienced his gracious power, they would no longer doubt his doctrine. (Sermon # 95)

The four Gospels record about thirty-five separate miracles that Jesus performed, including physical healings, raisings from the dead, exorcisms, and nature miracles (the multiplication of loaves and fish and calming of the seas). What is most important is they were performed as signs of hope and invitations to faith.

Jesus resisted any showmanship in his saving deeds, and when his actions did not elicit the intended faith, he was disappointed:

The Pharisees and Sadducees came, and to test him they asked him to show them a sign from heaven. He answered them, "When it is evening, you say, 'It will be fair weather; for the sky is red.' And in the morning, 'It will be stormy today, for the sky is red and threatening.' You know how to interpret the appearance of the sky, but you cannot interpret the signs of the times. An evil and adulterous generation seeks for a sign, but no sign shall be given to it except the sign of Jonah." So he left them and departed. (Mt. 16:1–4)

In John's Gospel Jesus gives the final positive word on his signs and wonders:

> If I am not doing the works of my Father, then do not believe in me; but if I do them, even though you do not believe in me, believe the works, that you may know and understand that the Father is in me and I am in the Father. (Jn. 10:37)

The Enemy

To underscore the fact that Jesus' healing ministry and miracles were not a philanthropic exercise but an overcoming of the effects of sin and Satan in the world, it is important to notice how these two realities — healing and exorcism — go together from the beginning of his ministry.

In the first chapter of Mark's Gospel, there is already a dramatic curing of a man possessed by a demon in the synagogue at Capernaum (Mk. 1:23–28). That same evening,

> ... at sundown, they brought to him all who were sick or possessed with demons. And the whole city was gathered together about the door. And he healed many who were sick with various diseases, and cast out many demons; and he would not permit the demons to speak, because they knew him. (Mk. 1:32–34)

In giving a summary of Jesus' ministry, Mark writes, "He went into their synagogues preaching the good news and expelling demons throughout the whole of Galilee"(Mk. 1:39).

Jesus' ministry, in fact, was launched with a confrontation, testing, and temptation by Satan himself. Mark speaks sparingly of this episode:

> The Spirit immediately drove him out into the wilderness. And he was in the wilderness forty days, tempted by Satan; and he was with the wild beasts; and the angels ministered to him. (Mk. 1:12–13)

Matthew, chapter 4, and Luke, chapter 4, both have a more elaborate narration of this episode with citations from the Old Testament. From their narrative we can deduce that the heart of the struggle was to tempt Jesus to use his power in his own self-interest, to provide himself with food, or to take an easier route for his messianic ministry than the one the Father had laid out for him.

Jesus rejected these temptations, but from that point on he was in a constant battle with Satan until the climactic event of the Cross in which Christ defeated Satan by seeming to be defeated himself. Awesome humility defeated awesome pride!

When Jesus taught about the Kingdom, he warned his hearers that being responsive and faithful was not merely a matter of good will but of spiritual combat with Satan. While good seed was being sown in their hearts by Christ, he warns, "Satan immediately comes and takes away the word which is sown in them" (Mk. 4:15). His Jewish hearers had been reared on the story of Genesis of the original loss of innocence and Satan's involvement. They knew that he was the Father of lies from the beginning and anxious to create estrangement between men and God.

Satan was also the architect of the final struggle that resulted in Jesus' death. Speaking of Judas and his decision to betray Jesus, John's Gospel says, "Satan entered into him" (Jn. 13:27).

Therefore in his earthly, pre-paschal ministry Jesus was not only proclaiming the arrival of God's kingdom and performing signs to validate his message, he was directly confronting Satan and the evil spirits to overcome all the evil and harm that they had brought to the human family from the beginning. This confrontation would reach its climax on the Cross where Jesus would overcome death — Satan's legacy to humankind:

> He himself likewise partook of the same nature, that through death he might destroy him who has the power of death, that is, the devil, and deliver all those who through fear of death were subject to life-long bondage. (Heb. 2:14–15)

Paul was true to the mystery and teaching of Jesus when he told his converts:

> Put on the whole armor of God, that you may be able to stand against the wiles of the devil. For we are not contending against flesh and blood, but against the principalities, against the powers, against the world rulers of this present darkness, against the spiritual hosts of wickedness in the heavenly places. (Eph. 6:11–12)

Minister of Compassion

It is difficult to find one single attribute to capture the person and the behavior of the pre-paschal Jesus, but perhaps "minister of compassion" does create a helpful synthesis of the many rich aspects of his earthly ministry.

Already in his inaugural sermon in the Synagogue of Nazareth Jesus identified himself with the Servant of God in Isaiah: "The Spirit of the Lord is upon me, because he has anointed me to preach good news to the poor. He has sent me to proclaim release to the captives and recovering of sight to the blind, to set at liberty those who are oppressed, to proclaim the acceptable year of the Lord" (Lk. 4:18–19).

In fulfillment of this Messianic call, Jesus associates himself with the outcasts and the sinners of his time, even sharing table fellowship with them for which he was criticized. His response is clear: "The Son of man came to seek and save the lost" (Lk. 19:10).

In the ultimate act of compassion, he claims and exercises the power to forgive sins. When, for example, curing the paralytic at Capernaum we read:

> When Jesus saw their faith, he said to the paralytic, "Child, your sins are forgiven." Now some of the scribes were sitting there, questioning in their hearts, "Why does this man speak like this? It is blasphemy! Who can forgive sins but God alone?" And immediately Jesus, perceiving in his spirit that they questioned like this within themselves, said to them, "Why do you question like this in your hearts? Which is easier, to say to the paralytic, 'Your sins are forgiven,'

or to say, 'Rise, take up your pallet and walk'? But that
you may know that the Son of man has authority on
earth to forgive sins" — he said to the paralytic — "I
say to you, rise, take up your pallet and go home."
And he rose, and immediately took up the pallet and
went out before them all; so that they were all amazed
and glorified God, saying, "We never saw anything
like this!" (Mk. 2:5–12)

As a minister of compassion, it was the person that mat-
tered to Jesus. He touched and healed lepers — even though
this was forbidden by Jewish law (Mk. 1:41). He embraced
little children even though the disciples wanted to chase
them away (Mk. 10:13–16). He wants to reveal to each person their own dignity in the eyes of God and that they are
truly beloved of God. This was why people, even sinners,
felt accepted in his presence.

His attitude in his encounters with the marginal-
ized is one of the best documented traits of the historical Jesus. On account of this he is spoken of as
being "in the company of sinners." One of the
New Testament descriptions of him was "a glut-
ton and a drunkard, a friend of tax collectors and
sinners!" (Mt. 11:19). In the message of Jesus the
coming of the Kingdom means the salvific coming of God precisely to publicans, prostitutes,
Samaritans, lepers, widows, children, the igno-
rant, gentiles, and the sick.[7]

Jesus was sensitive to those around him. He was patient with the dullness and incomprehension of his disciples. He wept when Lazarus, his friend, died. He reached out to the Samaritan woman at the well even when she was rude and dismissive to him (Jn. 4). He allowed the sinful woman to touch him (Lk. 7:36–39).

His teachings also reflect this dominant trait of compassion — he reveals his Father as a God of mercy and compassion in the parable of the prodigal son (Lk. 15:11–32). He performed deeds of compassion even when they seemed to violate the Law of the sabbath, saying, "The sabbath was made for man, not man for the sabbath" (Mk 2:27). He urged his followers to imitate the divine compassion in his parable of the Good Samaritan (Lk. 10).

Jesus lived in a male-dominated society and culture in which women were considered property of their father and then of their husband. Yet, in his relationships with them he manifests an attitude of serene welcome and respect. He clearly treasured his friendship with the sisters Mary and Martha of Bethany (Lk. 10:38–42). The Gospels report that women were in the company of the disciples and assisted them (Lk. 8:1–3). He holds the poor widow up as an example of true love of God (Mk. 12:41–44). He makes the sinful woman an example of the highest form of loving contrition and repentance (Lk. 7:36–50).

Finally, Jesus' compassion is highlighted in his teaching and example on the subject of forgiveness of enemies. Knowing that only forgiveness can short-circuit the spiral of vengeance and retaliation in which so many were caught, he said:

I say to you, love your enemies and pray for those
who persecute you, so that you may be sons of your
Father who is in heaven; for he makes his sun rise on
the evil and on the good, and sends rain on the just
and on the unjust. (Mt. 5:44–45)

He crowned this teaching with his own example. On
the cross, surrounded by his taunting enemies, he prays,
"Father, forgive them; for they know not what they do" (Lk.
23:34).

Surely, compassion is a unifying thread that runs
through the ministry of Jesus from its inauguration to its climax on the cross and is one of the reasons for his enduring
appeal over the centuries, even to those who do not fully
understand his mystery.

Consciousness, Identity, Claims

The New Testament witnesses to Jesus' consciousness of
being "the Son." This awareness and intimate relationship
with God as "my Father" gave the direction and purpose to
his life and ministry. Without it the whole drama of his ministry was senseless. This intuitive awareness and consciousness was central to his person and ministry.

It is a more modern question as to how and when this
"consciousness" arose. This preoccupation comes perhaps
from the dominance of psychology in our modern culture.
The Scriptures do not give us all the answers in this area we
moderns might like.

It is possible that Jesus' full personal awareness of his
divine filiation was a gradual and growing experience. Perhaps a hint of this intuitive consciousness is given when the

twelve-year-old boy Jesus says to Mary, "Did you not know that I must be in my Father's house?" (Lk. 2:49).

At Jesus' Baptism, Mark reports that Jesus himself heard, "You are my beloved Son, with whom I am well pleased" (Mk. 1:11). This could have been a highlight moment of this ongoing consciousness and awareness that strengthened him for the public ministry he was about to embrace.

Theologians often speak of an "implicit Christology" regarding the pre-paschal Jesus. He did not wish to reveal his fullest identity or make claims at a time and in a setting in which such claims could so easily be and were misinterpreted in earthly and political terms. Jesus shows a great reserve in speaking of himself and was constantly trying to correct false ideas of Messiahship imposed upon him by others. One author puts it well:

> Jesus had a problem. If we presume at this point that Jesus knew himself to be the Son of God and wanted to reveal this, he had to do so in such a manner so as to distinguish himself from God (the Father) and simultaneously uphold the truth that there is only one God. This is precisely what Jesus did through his words and actions, and he did so in very creative and imaginative ways.[8]

Whatever claims Jesus makes about himself are subtle and indirect. He does not ever directly call himself "God," which would have created total confusion at that moment in the world of strict Jewish monotheism.

His contemporaries saw him and addressed him as "Rabbi/Teacher." This title is used of him 59 times in the Gospels. Yet, he clearly exceeds so simple a designation:

They questioned among themselves, saying, "What is this? A new teaching! With authority he commands even the unclean spirits, and they obey him." (Mk. 1:27)

Unlike Rabbis of his day, Jesus not only interpreted and expounded the ancient Law/Torah of Israel, but he took it upon himself to change it, and he did so on his own personal authority. This is reflected in the series of antitheses of Matthew chapter 5: "You have heard that it was said (he quotes the Jewish law). . . . But I say to you that. . . ." And he modifies this Law. A most striking example is his personal reversal of the Mosaic tradition allowing divorce (Mk. 10:2–12). Jesus of Nazareth makes the enormous claim that his authority exceeds that of Moses. All of this manifests an exceptional claim to an extraordinary knowledge of God's will and an authority to interpret it.

Moreover, Jesus' actions and attitude conveyed an unheard of sense of transcendent authority:

Either by what he said or what he did (or both), Jesus claimed authority over the observance of the sabbath (Mk. 2:23–28; 3:1–5), the temple (Mk. 11:15–17, 22–33), and the law. A unique sacredness attached to that day, place, and code. . . . Thus, in proclaiming the present divine rule, Jesus repeatedly and in a variety of ways claimed or at least implied a personal authority that can be described as setting himself on a par with God.[9]

His disciples came to recognize Jesus as Messiah (Mk. 8:27–30). Jesus accepted this Jewish designation but discouraged his disciples from using it because, at that moment, for the people, it had more of a political overtone as the King who would free Palestine from the political domination of Rome. Jesus' Messiahship was much different and much more than that narrow role.

One of the strategies Jesus used to express his implicit Christology was the mysterious title "Son of Man." It occurs on Jesus' lips 69 times in the Synoptic Gospels and is found 12 times in John. In the ears of those who heard him in this pre-paschal situation it was a subtle and wonderful invitation to look more deeply at his person and mission in new terms.

"Son of Man" also suited Jesus' teaching noted earlier about the two stages of the coming of the Kingdom. It highlighted the ultimate and final coming of the Kingdom. Jesus' reference was to the Book of Daniel, chapter 7, where we read of a mysterious figure who is associated with Yahweh and shares his sovereignty:

> I saw in the night visions, and behold, with the clouds of heaven there came one like the son of man, and he came to the Ancient of Days and was presented before him. And to him was given dominion and glory and kingdom, that all peoples, nations, and languages should serve him; his dominion is an everlasting dominion, which shall not pass

away, and his kingdom one that shall not be destroyed. (Dan. 7:13–14)

Jesus speaks of himself as "Son of Man" in three ways: to refer to his current humble situation, in connection with his future suffering and death (where he joins it with the figure of the suffering Servant of Isaiah), and for his coming in glory at the end of time. Because the early Church almost totally dropped the title, we can have confidence that Jesus himself was the originator of its use and did so as an implicit claim to his unique and divine dignity and authority.

In conclusion, we can say that an overwhelming combination of factors in Jesus' person, words, and behavior point to a transcendent dignity and authority that was difficult to articulate in the pre-paschal situation. He clearly does not fit neatly into any Jewish category of the time. As one modern Jewish scholar has noted: "I am more than ever certain that a great place belongs to him in Israel's history of faith and that this place cannot be described by any of the usual categories" (Martin Buber).

It is this strong, if implicit, Christology of the pre-paschal Jesus that begs for further answers and clarification that could only come in the post-paschal situation. For this reason, Archbishop Angelo Amato prefers the term "Open Christology":

Open Christology would be pre-paschal Christology, that is the incipient faith of the disciples which has already the fundamental elements on which full faith can be founded and which remains "open" to its completion in the resurrection, the decisive event of illumination of the whole mystery of Christ.[10]

While Jesus' claims and identity were expressed in cautious and implicit ways, his meaning was not lost on many of the Jewish religious authorities of his time. Sadly, they were not "open" to further illumination but rejected him outright. Significantly, and showing that they well understood the implications of his "implicit Christology," they condemned him precisely for blasphemy. At his trial, the high priest said: "'You have heard his blasphemy. What is your decision?' And they all condemned him as deserving death" (Mk. 14:64). We may say then that Jesus was condemned precisely because of his consciousness, identity, and claims.

The Mother

We cannot leave our treatment of the pre-paschal Jesus without giving attention to his mother, Mary of Nazareth. As every human person is greatly influenced and affected by their parents, so was Jesus. Certainly there was even a physical resemblance to her from whom alone he took his human nature. But more important was the spiritual presence of this uniquely graced woman in his first thirty years of life. There is here a beautiful mystery that is mostly unknown to us.

It was Mary's *Fiat* — "Let it be to me according to your word" (Lk. 1:38) — that made possible the saving ministry of Jesus. She is thus not only the physical mother but also the first of Christian believers and the first disciple. St. Augustine wrote:

It was for her a greater thing to have been Christ's
disciple then to have been his mother, and she was
more blessed in her discipleship than in her motherhood. (Sermon #25)

In fact, however, her motherhood and faith were inextricably linked. As Elizabeth exclaimed to her, "Blessed is
she who believed that there would be a fulfillment of what
was spoken to her from the Lord" (Lk. 1:45).

The prelude to Jesus' birth was the Annunciation to Mary:

Do not be afraid, Mary, for you have found favor
with God. And behold, you will conceive in your
womb and bear a son, and you shall call his name
Jesus. He will be great, and will be called the Son of
the Most High; and the Lord God will give him the
throne of his father David, and he will reign over
the house of Jacob for ever; and of his kingdom
there will be no end." (Lk. 1:30–33)

Having given her free consent, Mary's soul is thereafter
filled with the humble grateful joy of the perfect disciple:

He has regarded the low estate of his handmaiden.
For behold, henceforth all generations will call me
blessed; for he who is mighty has done great things
for me, and holy is his name. (Lk. 1:48–49)

Thus Mary, in God's eternal wisdom and plan, becomes
the necessary partner of Christ in the work of mankind's salvation. Already in the second century St. Irenaeus dared to

call her "the cause of salvation for herself and for the whole human race."

This association of Mary with Jesus' salvific ministry was not limited to his birth from her. As the Second Vatican Council teaches in its Dogmatic Constitution on the Church:

> This union of the Mother with the Son in the work of salvation is made manifest from the time of Christ's virginal conception up to his death.... The blessed Virgin advanced in her pilgrimage of faith, and faithfully persevered in her union with her son unto the cross. (*Lumen Gentium*, 57, 58)

She appears at different moments of his pre-paschal ministry expressing her indomitable faith in him, as at the wedding feast of Cana, thus producing his first miracle (Jn. 2:1–11). Finally, she was present at the foot of the Cross to share in his saving sacrifice,

> uniting herself with a maternal heart with His sacrifice, and lovingly consenting to the immolation of this Victim which she herself had brought forth. (*Lumen Gentium*, 58)

The more one penetrates the full mystery of Christ, the more one inevitably venerates the Virgin Mary, who had so singular and unique a role in God's saving plan for the human family. As the early Church instinctively gathered around her after the Ascension (Acts 1:13–14), so it has continued to seek her powerful intercession in the centuries that have unfolded and never ceased to praise the wonders God worked in and through her.[11]

Endnotes — Chapter 4

[1] See John Riches, *The World of Jesus: First Century Judaism in Crisis* (New York: Cambridge University Press, 1990).

[2] John Meier, *A Marginal Jew*, Vol. 1 (New York: Doubleday, 1991). See Chapter 11, "A Chronology of Jesus' Life," pp. 372–433.

[3] Karl Rahner, *The Eternal Year* (Montreal: Palm Publishers, 1994), p. 97.

[4] John Meier: *A Marginal Jew*, Vol. 2 (New York: Doubleday, 1991), p. 239. See chapter 14, "The Kingdom of God."

[5] Raymond Brown, *An Introduction to New Testament Christology* (New York: Paulist Press), p. 61; see also chapter 5.

[6] For a full treatment of this topic see Reginald Fuller, *Interpreting the Miracles* (Philadelphia: Westminster Press, 1963), and Renè Latourelle, *The Miracles of Jesus and the Theology of Miracles* (New York: Paulist Press, 1988).

[7] Angelo Amato, *Jesù Il Signore* (Bologna: Edizioni Dehoniane, 2003), p. 169.

[8] Thomas Weinandy, *Jesus the Christ* (Huntington IN: Our Sunday Visitor, 2003), p. 30.

[9] Gerald O'Collins, *Christology — A Biblical, Historical and Systematic Study of Jesus* (New York: Oxford University Press), pp. 59–60.

[10] Angelo Amato, Jesù Il Signore (Bologna: Edizioni Dehoniane, 2003), p. 162.

[11] For further reflection on Mary's role read: Pope Paul VI, "Apostolic Exhortation on Devotion to Blessed Virgin Mary," 1974, and Pope John Paul II, *Mother of the Redeemer*, 1987, both available from USCCB Publications, Washington, D.C.

CHAPTER 5

THE PASCHAL MYSTERY: JESUS' DEATH AND RESURRECTION

Initially, it would seem that Jesus' mission focused on the spiritual renewal of Israel by his teachings, his miracles, and his call to faith and conversion. All of these were a means of manifesting the breaking into history of God's reign and saving love. Jesus strenuously devoted himself to this mission, moving from town to town.

A change of perspective, however, begins to occur — reflected, for example, in chapter 8 of Mark's Gospel. Jesus begins to identify his mission with that of the Suffering Servant of Isaiah (chapters 52 and 53), and we find the first of a series of predictions on his lips, "The Son of man must suffer many things, and be rejected by the elders and the chief priests and the scribes, and be killed" (Mk. 8:31).

Factors that led to this change of perspective certainly included the strident opposition to Jesus by the religious authorities that began almost from the beginning of his ministry. After his cure of a man on the Sabbath in the synagogue, in which Jesus directly confronted the religious authorities, we read, "The Pharisees went out, and immediately held council with the Herodians against him, how to destroy him" (Mk. 3:6).

Fr. Gerald O'Collins, S.J., writes of this transition:

> At some point Jesus began to anticipate and accept his violent death. He saw his ministry as standing, at least partially, in continuity with the prophets.... In his prophetic role, Jesus expected to die a martyr's death and apparently expected that to happen in Jerusalem (Lk. 11:42–49; Mk. 12:1–2)... his entry into Jerusalem and protest in cleansing the temple... were a final, dangerous challenge to the religious authorities in the city and the power they exercised through the temple.[1]

Despite this change of focus and perspective there is also a strong continuity between the early and last stages of Jesus' ministry:

> A straight line led from his serving ministry to his suffering death... there was a basis in Jesus' life for the saying, "The Son of man also came not to be served but to serve, and to give his life as a ransom for many" (Mk. 10:45). He who had shown himself as the servant of all was ready to become the victim for all.... Part of the reason why Jesus' ministry led to his crucifixion stemmed from the fact that he faithfully and scandalously served the lost, the godless, and the alienated of his society. The physician

who came to call and cure the unrighteous eventually died as their representative.[2]

The coming of Jesus, the Son of God, into the human arena is above all else the unfolding of the drama of human salvation — God's loving intervention in human history to undo the tragic realities of sin and death. Jesus' pre-paschal ministry begins this process, but his death and resurrection were the necessary climax of this saving event.

The Last Supper

John's Gospel begins the narrative of this pivotal event with these words:

> Before the feast of the Passover, Jesus knew that his hour had come to depart out of this world to the Father, having loved his own who were in the world, he loved them to the end. (Jn. 13:1)

This Johannine theme of "the hour" underlines the centrality of this moment for Jesus' life and ministry. At the Supper, Jesus is gathered with the Twelve — the representatives of the new spiritual Israel that was being formed — the Church — that will be the result of his ministry.

With them he celebrates the Jewish Passover Supper ritual and gives it a new dimension focused on his free offering of himself as the new Paschal Lamb.

> As they were eating, he took bread, and blessed, and broke it, and gave it to them, and said, "Take; this is my body." And he took a chalice, and when he had

given thanks he gave it to them, and they all drank
of it. And he said to them, "This is my blood of the
covenant, which is poured out for many." (Mk.
14:22–24)

Here Jesus, the High Priest of the New Covenant, is
truly offering himself, in keeping with the Father's plan and
will, as the Saving Victim for the salvation of mankind.

This offering would then unfold through the hands of
his executioners in a bloody and violent fashion. But all its
meaning and power derive from that free self-oblation at the
Supper table. It is the ultimate act of love — the gift of his
life for all his human brothers and sisters. In these simple
words and gestures in the Upper Room were laid the foundations of the Church's later understanding of Jesus' death as
expiation, propitiation, and the means of humanity's recon-
ciliation with God the Father.

Who Was Responsible?

Historically, we may say that two agents bear responsibility
for the historical condemnation and execution of Jesus of
Nazareth:

1. Some of the Jewish religious leadership

They came to see Jesus as disrespectful towards the Law
(Mk. 2:23), disrespectful to the Temple (Mt. 26:61), and
making blasphemous assertions about himself (Mt. 26:64).
For these reasons, they judged him guilty of death in a meeting of the Sanhedrin, the Jewish ruling body.

This responsibility is narrow and cannot be extended. As the Second Vatican Council stated in its Declaration on the Relation of the Church to Non-Christian Religions:

> True, the Jewish authorities and those who followed their lead pressed for the death of Christ (cf. John 19:6); still, what happened in His passion cannot be charged against all the Jews, without distinction, then alive, nor against the Jews of today. (*Nostra Aetate*, 4)

2. Pilate

Because the Sanhedrin did not have authority to put anyone to death, they brought Jesus to Pilate, the Roman governor in charge of Palestine. They suggested that his messianic claims were a threat to the emperor. Pilate acceded to the clamor of the crowd and sentenced Jesus to death.

In the wider view, however, of God's plan and saving purpose, we realize that, because of our sins, we are all responsible for Christ's death on the cross. All of us bear responsibility to the extent that through sin we have contributed to causing Christ's death for us as the victim who expiates our sins.

It is the sin of humanity from the beginning that led to the tragedy of Calvary. Man's free choice, beginning in Adam, to reject God's will and to disobey His commands led to the situation of estrangement from God. It was God's love for his creatures that inspired the salvific strategy of Jesus' sufferings and death so that through him we might again be reconciled with God.

The Gospel Accounts

Much of the text of the four Gospels is taken up by the detailed narration of Jesus' Passion.[3] Of these large segments, Cardinal Kasper notes:

> The Passion tradition is clearly an old and selfcontained element of the New Testament tradition. There can be no doubt that it is close to the historical events. . . . More important than questions of historical detail, however, is the fact that the Passion tradition clearly reveals the influence of theological interests. These may be apologetic, dogmatic, or devotional, and they show that the Passion narratives were intended not just as narratives, but as preaching. They already interpret the Passion in the light of the Resurrection. The Passion is presented as the sufferings of the Messiah, the sufferings of the Just One, the fulfillment of the Old Testament, and therefore the fulfillment of the will of God. The Song of the Suffering Servant (Is. 53) and Psalms 22 and 69 had a deep influence on these accounts.[4]

These accounts begin with the Agony in the Garden and the narrative of Jesus' obedient surrender to the Father's will ("not my will, but yours be done" [Lk. 22:42]) and continue with the betrayal by Judas, the arrest and trials before the Sanhedrin and Pilate, the condemnation to death, the scourging, the crucifixion, and the death of Jesus.

Taken together, the narrative gives us seven "words" from the Cross — the last words of Jesus. They are words of surrender, of forgiveness, and of mercy that sum up the whole life and ministry of Jesus.

The Mystery of the Cross

St. Paul put it simply, "We preach Christ crucified" (1 Cor. 1:23). The cross is the ultimate criterion of any true Christology. It is the supreme paradox that is the center of Christian belief — it establishes Christian identity. No wonder the cross is placed on the steeple of every Christian Church and is traced on the forehead of every newly baptized Christian.

The Crucifixion is above all else the ultimate manifestation of the merciful love of God. Paul exclaims, "I live by faith in the Son of God, who loved me and gave himself for me" (Gal. 2:20). Through it we have come to know "the breadth and length and height and depth" (Eph. 3:18) of Christ's love.

The Paschal Mystery of Christ's suffering, death, and resurrection is the rock on which Christianity is founded and its most characteristic element when compared with all other world religions. The Resurrection is precisely the raising of the Crucified one whose "glorious wounds" are the pledges of our salvation.

So difficult, however, is it for the human mind to accept this awesome reality of divine abnegation that the Koran, the holy book of Islam, dismisses it as an "illusion," saying Jesus was "neither killed, nor crucified" (Surah 4:157). Other major religions, such as Hinduism and Buddhism, find it equally incomprehensible.

Yet, as St. Paul wrote:

> We preach Christ Crucified, a stumbling block to
> Jews and folly to Gentiles, but to those who are
> called, both Jews and Greeks, Christ the power of
> God and the wisdom of God. For the foolishness of
> God is wiser than men, and the weakness of God is
> stronger than men. (1 Cor. 1:23–25)

The Crucifixion is also the absolute criterion for understanding Jesus and Christianity. This is so because it brings together the essential realities that an integral Christianity must include:

- The reality of sin
- Our personal accountability
- Authentic personal guilt
- Just punishment for sin
- Divine judgment
- Expiation for sin
- God's saving love

For some decades many of these essential realities have been downplayed or ignored in catechesis or preaching. The result has been what some commentators have called "Christianity Light." To discover the *true Jesus* is to discover the *Crucified Savior* and to understand all the elements involved in the drama of our salvation.

Ironically, a secular source like *Time* magazine noted:

> The large proportion of Christians really doesn't
> think of Jesus' death. . . . You go straight from Palm
> Sunday to Easter without passing go . . . Americans

tended not to linger on the agony of Jesus. It was more "friend of my soul, he walks with me and talks with me"... that suggests a Christianity with a large hole in it. "The cross is at the center of Christianity, and we know that it was at the center of Jesus' own thinking," says John Stott, an Anglican preacher... "I could never myself believe in God if it were not for the Cross.... In the real world of pain, how could one worship a God who was immune to it?" (*Time*, April 12, 2004)

If Christianity faces a "crisis of relevance," as some have asserted, then an antidote may be found precisely in the message of the Cross. As the great Protestant theologian Jürgen Moltmann has written, "Only reflection upon the cross leads to the clarification of what can be called Christian identity and Christian relevance."[5] In a world of guilt, pain, tragedy, sorrow, and death the Cross is the interpretative key to unlock the mysteries of human existence.

Soteriology

This term — the theology of salvation — represents the efforts of the Church to try to understand and explain the significance of Jesus' suffering and death.

It took time for a soteriology to develop. The cross represented a radical reversal of popular Jewish messianic expectation. In fact, death on a cross meant being cursed by God:

Christ has redeemed us from the curse of the law, having become a curse for us — for it is written,

"Cursed be every one who hangs on a tree" [Deut. 21:23]. (Gal. 3:13)

The earliest soteriology is sparse and sober. Paul, in Corinthians, transmits the simple faith he learned from the Jerusalem Church:

> For I delivered to you as of first importance what I also received, that Christ died for our sins in accordance with the Scriptures. (1 Cor. 15:3)

The Scriptures referred to here are especially the passages from Isaiah about the mysterious Suffering Servant of Yahweh who would carry the guilt of all and by his sufferings redeem all. These passages become critical for the early Jewish Christians in helping them understand and accept Christ's sufferings. A frequent refrain became what is preserved in Luke's Gospel: "Was it not necessary that the Christ should suffer these things and enter into his glory?" (Lk. 24:26). Thus, before more deeply interpreting and explaining these events — which is the task of Soteriology — they found in their Jewish faith and tradition an interpretative key to help them with this process.

As decades went on and the community prayed and reflected on these mysteries, deeper insights developed on the meaning of Jesus' suffering and death. The various Gospels — while presenting a fairly uniform narrative of the events — give them a different interpretation according to the goals of each particular Gospel:

- **Matthew/Mark** — writing for a Jewish audience — emphasize Jesus as the true Suffering Servant of Isaiah who is abandoned by his followers, condemned by his countrymen, and even forsaken by God — thus giving his life as a ransom.

- **Luke**, however, writing for a gentile audience represents the suffering Jesus as a Healer and Savior. He reassures Peter, "I will pray for you," he heals the ear of the soldier who arrests him when Peter severs it, and he forgives those who crucify him and promises the thief on the cross paradise.

- **John's** suffering Jesus is clearly the Divine Son who finds his "glory" precisely in this awesome act of love for the Father and humanity: "Now is my soul troubled. And what shall I say? 'Father, save me from this hour'? No, for this purpose I have come to this hour. Father, glorify your name" (Jn. 12:27).

Taken together, these Gospel accounts give a rich portrait of the Suffering Christ and begin to unlock some of the mystery of the Passion.

The early Church, reflected especially in the Pauline writings and the Letter to the Hebrews, carried this process of understanding further. The early Church's Soteriology is profound and includes the following elements, which are interwoven in the teaching of Paul and John and which can only be briefly summarized here:

1. The Passion as the Supreme Manifestation of the Love of God:

In this the love of God was made manifest among us, that God sent his only-begotten Son into the world, so that we might live through him. In this is love, not that we loved God but that he loved us and sent his Son to be the expiation for our sins. (1 Jn. 4:9–10)

It is important to highlight this central aspect of Christian Soteriology because sometimes the Cross has been presented primitively as a means of appeasing an angry God. The Cross in the biblical view is a gratuitous act of love by God — he makes it an altar of propitiation and pardon for us. Through it he pardons and reconciles humanity to himself.

God shows his love for us in that while we were yet sinners Christ died for us. Since, therefore, we are now justified by his blood, much more shall we be saved by him from the wrath of God. (Rom. 5:8–9)

2. Obedient Victimhood

Jesus' love for the Father leads him to willingly accept the divine plan and submit to a painful and ignominious death to thus undo the primeval pride and disobedience of humans.

For as by one man's disobedience many were made sinners, so by one man's obedience many will be made righteous. (Rom. 5:19)

In the infinite wisdom of God, the humility and obedience of Jesus was able to undo the effects of the pride and
disobedience of mankind.

3. Reconciliation

A major element of Pauline Soteriology. This dimension presumes a pre-existing alienation between God and
humans. Even though God is the aggrieved party, he takes
the initiative to end the separation and unite us to himself:

> All this is from God, who through Christ reconciled
> us to himself and gave us the ministry of reconcili-
> ation; that is, in Christ God was reconciling the
> world to himself, not counting their trespasses
> against them, and entrusting to us the message of
> reconciliation. So we are ambassadors for Christ,
> God making his appeal through us. We beg you on
> behalf of Christ, be reconciled to God. For our sake
> he made him to be sin who knew no sin, so that in
> him we might become the righteousness of God. (2
> Cor. 5:18–21)

4. Atonement

The letter to the Hebrews especially highlights this
dimension of Jesus' Passion and Death. From chapters 7 to
10, the author builds on the Old Testament's familiar
imagery of Priest and Victim to show the superiority of the
New Covenant in which God's Son, Jesus himself, is both
Priest and Victim.

By the time of the writing of Hebrews, the Christian
community was regularly celebrating the Eucharist in which,

as St. Paul had taught, "you proclaim the Lord's death until he comes" (1 Cor. 11:26). Perhaps the Church's liturgical celebration led to the deepening of these particular insights on the Passion as the exercise of Christ's priesthood and the Eucharist as the re-presentation of his perfectly atoning sacrifice.

> But when Christ appeared as a high priest of the good things that have come, then through the greater and more perfect tent (not made with hands, that is, not of this creation) he entered once for all into the holy place, taking not the blood of goats and calves but his own blood, thus securing an eternal redemption. For if the sprinkling of defiled persons with the blood of goats and bulls and with the ashes of a heifer sanctifies for the purification of the flesh, how much more shall the blood of Christ, who through the eternal spirit offered himself without blemish to God, purify your conscience from dead works to serve the living God. (Heb. 9:11–14)

Jesus' priestly sacrifice has thus made atonement making us again one with God in grace and justice.

The Resurrection

Good Friday and Holy Saturday were not the final word of the Christ Event. The awesome *kenosis* (self-emptying) that carried him from prior divine life to the Incarnation and to the abasement of the Cross led to his glorious exultation. He:

... emptied himself, taking the form of a servant, being born in the likeness of men. And being found in human form he humbled himself and became obedient unto death, even death on a cross. Therefore God has highly exalted him and bestowed on him the name which is above every name, that at the name of Jesus every knee should bow, in heaven and on earth and under the earth, and every tongue confess that Jesus Christ is Lord, to the glory of God the Father. (Phil. 2:7–11)

The exaltation of Jesus includes his rising from dead, his humanity being transfigured, and his enthronement at the Father's right hand forever.

The process begins in the cold tomb of Holy Saturday night when God raises his mangled body to life — the Resurrection. Each year we recapture that moment when, in the dark of the Easter Vigil, the new fire is enkindled and the Paschal Candle, symbol of the Risen Christ, is lit.

St. Paul emphasizes the centrality of this event as the primary criterion of the truth of the Christian message: "If Christ has not been raised, then our preaching is in vain and your faith is in vain" (1 Cor. 15:14).

Fr. O'Collins has expanded on this statement trenchantly:

At the very origins of Christianity we do not find some general truth (God is Father of us all) or some basic moral injunction to "love" . . . but a specific message proclaimed. . . . The crucified Jesus has been raised from the dead. The early Christian witness intended to make a factually informative statement about something new which God had brought about after Jesus' death . . . the original and essential point of the Easter message centered on this: God has done something to and for the dead Jesus — raising him from the dead to a transformed and definitive life of glory![6]

As we review and contemplate the Resurrection of Jesus, which is at one and the same time a fact, a dogma, and a mystery, we need to consider a number of elements.

1. The Post-Calvary Context and Situation

This is poignantly expressed in the words of the sad disciples on the way to Emmaus on Easter afternoon: "We had hoped he was the one to redeem Israel" (Lk. 24:21). The stunned grief, despair, and hopelessness of the disciples is narrated by all the Gospels.

Jesus' death was the end of their hopes because Jesus' message was so related to his person that it could not survive after his death. His message stood or fell with his person. In him the promised kingdom had seemed to dawn. But now he had been executed as a condemned criminal and was abandoned by all except Mary, John, and a few women. His whole project seemed to be an utter failure.

The Gospels all narrate the lack of credulity of the disciples and their initial refusal to believe any report of Jesus rising: "When they heard that he was alive and had been seen by her [Mary Magdalene], they would not believe it" (Mk. 16:11).

2. The Empty Tomb

There was no eyewitness for the actual moment of Jesus' resurrection.

What stood as the powerful symbol of that mystery was precisely the empty tomb. The discovery of the empty tomb is the first step on the road to faith in the Resurrection. All four Gospels describe the women coming to the tomb early on Easter morning and finding it empty.

The empty tomb is the link between the Crucifixion and the Resurrection. Jesus' followers helped place his body in the tomb (Mk. 15:42–47) on Good Friday. On the following Sunday, the body was no longer there — what had happened?

By itself, the empty tomb is an ambiguous phenomenon. Early Jewish anti-Christian polemic did not deny it but claimed the body was stolen (Mt. 28:11–15). For one, however, who was disposed, the empty tomb could be the catalyst for faith as it was for the beloved disciple (Jn. 20:8).

The importance of the empty tomb is that it powerfully expresses the personal continuity between the pre-paschal Jesus and the Risen Lord. It is precisely the Crucified One who has been raised.

3. The Appearances

The very earliest written statement that we have about the Resurrection involves a list of Jesus' appearances to individuals or groups:

He appeared to Cephas, then to the Twelve. Then he appeared to more than five hundred brethren at

one time, most of whom are still alive, though some
have fallen asleep. Then he appeared to James, then
to all the apostles. Last of all, as to one untimely
born, he appeared to me. (1 Cor. 15:5–8)

It was precisely the appearances that led the first Christians to accept the reality of Jesus' resurrection. In the quote
from 1 Cor. 15 above, the realism is noteworthy. Paul is
clearly speaking of events that were objective, factual, and
well-known. He repeats the word "seen" to emphasize the
true bodily reality of the Risen Christ.

Other Gospel accounts further emphasize the tangible
reality of the Risen Jesus. He says to the disciples, "'See my
hands and my feet, that it is I myself; handle me, and see; for
a spirit has not flesh and bones as you see that I have.' And
when he had said this he showed them his hands and his
feet" (Lk. 24:39–40). He went on to eat in their presence
(verses 42–43). John also speaks of Thomas touching the
wounds of his hands (Jn. 20:27–28).

Both Paul's early accounts and the Gospel narrations
insist on the testimony of eyewitnesses — specific and
known individuals whose personal experience qualifies them
to be witnesses of Jesus' resurrection. Significantly, when it
was necessary to choose a new Apostle to replace Judas
within the ranks of the Twelve, the Apostles required, as a
condition, that the one chosen be able to witness to Jesus'
resurrection (Acts 1:22).

Though the Scriptures clearly witness to a true bodily
resurrection, it needs to be emphasized that this was not
the mere resuscitation of a dead body but a resurrection to
a new and glorified body in which Jesus is "the first fruits

of those who have fallen asleep" (1 Cor. 15:20). This was the beginning of the unique transformation of the dead that he himself had preached about in his earthly ministry (Mt. 22:23–33). Jesus' rising is not merely a personal vindication or exaltation, but the first step in a process in which God's creative plan of life for all humankind will be realized.

> The Resurrection was no mere resuscitation of Jesus to ordinary life. When the Risen Jesus appeared, he was not easily recognizable even to those who knew him well (for example, Mary Magdalene and Simon Peter). He could pass through locked doors, cover distances instantaneously, and yet he still pointed to his body as real. Thus there is no evidence whatsoever that early preaching ever involved anything other than a bodily resurrection that involved tremendous transformation.[7]

There are many similarities in the four Gospel descriptions of the appearances that confirm the ancient nature and authenticity of the oral traditions from which they came. Yet, each writer felt free to adapt or emphasize aspects that are of particular significance to his community. Luke, for instance, makes a link with the Eucharist. The Risen Jesus is recognized in the "breaking of the bread" — a clear reference to the Eucharist the early Christians were already celebrating (Lk. 24:30–31, 35). Matthew, who is the evangelist of the Church's mission, includes the injunction of the Risen Jesus to his disciples to go and proclaim the good news to all peoples (Mt. 28:18–19).

4. *The Easter* Kerygma

The technical term *kerygma* refers to an announcement or proclamation, such as would be made in ancient times by a herald or messenger. The truth of the Resurrection became the essential content of the early Church's proclamation or *kerygma* because in it the saving action of God was most powerfully revealed. It was the central subject of the preaching of the Apostles and the early Church.

The Acts of the Apostles, which describes the earliest preaching of the Christian church, is full of versions of this early *kerygma*. It often seemed to include four elements:

- The human rejection/condemnation of Jesus
- The action of God the Father in raising his dead body
- The witness of the Apostles
- Some preliminary theological explanation (e.g., he was "delivered up according to the definite plan and foreknowledge of God" [Acts 2: 23])

The *kerygma* and the early preaching gradually teased out many more implications of Jesus' Resurrection as the Spirit helped the community to understand it. But basic and central to all these developments was the conviction that God had acted definitively in the person of his Son, Jesus Christ, and that therefore he was the only way to salvation. Peter expresses it powerfully:

This is the stone which was rejected by you builders, but which has become the cornerstone. And there

is salvation in no one else, for there is no other
name under heaven given among men by which we
must be saved. (Acts 4:11–12)

It is important to emphasize the Easter *kerygma* and its objective factual message about Jesus' true victory over death in
our moment of history because there is a great temptation in
our culture to relegate the spiritual to a subjective reality, a
matter of personal feelings or choice.

This point has been expressed well by the German theologian, Fr. Karl Rahner:

> Modern man has the unexpressed prejudice that
> anything "religious" is merely an affair of feelings,
> of the heart — something that we must bring about
> by ourselves; something therefore that involves the
> difficulties and unreality of the heart's thoughts and
> moods.
>
> Easter tells us that *God has done something.* "This
> is the work of the Lord — it is marvelous in our
> eyes." God has raised his Son from the dead; God
> has conquered death. He has done this not merely
> in the realm of inwardness, but in the actuality of
> the world, the body, in history far from all mere
> thought and mere sentiments.[8]

Rediscovering the Easter *kerygma* should give new
dynamism to the Church's missionary spirit that must
always be one of her essential characteristics. The Church
has a message about Jesus, the unique Savior, which she

must proclaim. She does not do so in a triumphalistic or patronizing way, but humbly offering to others the message of hope she has received:

> In your hearts reverence Christ as Lord. Always be prepared to make a defense to anyone who calls you to account for the hope that is in you, yet do it with gentleness and reverence. (1 Pet. 3:15–16)

The Easter Message is always actual and contemporary. It is the message of hope for which all people yearn. But this message of hope is rooted in a person — Jesus of Nazareth, who by his death and resurrection has become the Savior of the world.

Endnotes — Chapter 5

[1] Gerald O'Collins, *Christology: A Biblical, Historical and Systematic Study of Jesus* (New York: Oxford University Press, 1995), p. 68.

[2] Ibid., p. 76.

[3] A valuable analysis of the Gospel accounts of the Passion is Fr. Raymond Brown, *The Death of the Messiah*, 2 volumes (New York: Doubleday, 1994). For a relevant, theological commentary, see Gerald O'Collins, S.J., *The Calvary Christ* (Philadelphia: Westminster Press, 1977).

[4] Walter Kasper, *Jesus the Christ* (New York: Paulist Press, 1977), p. 115.

[5] Jürgen Moltmann, *The Crucified God* (New York: Harper and Row, 1974), p. 7.

[6] G. O'Collins, *Interpreting Jesus* (New York: Paulist Press, 1983), pp 112–113.

[7] Raymond Brown, "Jesus Really Rose," *St. Anthony Messenger*, April 1994, p. 13.

[8] Karl Rahner, *The Eternal Year* (Montreal: Palm Publishers, 1964), p. 88.

CHAPTER 6

CHRISTOLOGY BEGINS: THE EARLY CHURCH

Jesus Christ was encountered and followed right up to his death and resurrection by his disciples. This Christ Event was therefore first and primarily experiential — it was something that was lived and experienced. After Jesus' resurrection and ascension, however, this saving event had to be communicated, explained, and proclaimed. We have already seen how this began to happen in the Easter *kerygma*.

It is with this practical need that in a certain sense Christology — a systematic, conceptual presentation of the mystery of Jesus — really begins. This Christology is driven primarily by evangelistic and pastoral concerns: the community needs to express and proclaim its faith in the saving Christ Event they have experienced. Moreover, they have been commissioned by the Risen Christ to bring the good news to others. To do so, they need to develop terms, titles, and concepts that can try to express the mystery of Jesus Christ to others who have not shared their actual experiences.

As we consider this development, which took many decades, two things need to be kept in mind:

1. *This development of Christology is not a merely human, rational process.*

The guiding force of this development is the Holy Spirit. Jesus said, "I will ask the Father, and he will give you another Counselor, to be with you for ever, even the Spirit of truth" (Jn. 14:16). The post-Pentecost community was deeply conscious of the presence of the Spirit in the development and understanding of its Christological faith. Saint Paul wrote to one of his first communities, "No one can say 'Jesus is Lord' except in the Holy Spirit" (1 Cor. 12:3).

Further explaining the Spirit's role, Paul asserted:

> God has revealed to us through the Spirit. For the Spirit searches everything, even the depths of God. For what person knows a man's thoughts except the spirit of the man which is in him? So also no one comprehends the thoughts of God except the Spirit of God. Now we have received not the spirit of the world, but the spirit which is from God, that we might understand the gifts bestowed on us by God. And we impart this in words not taught by human wisdom but taught by the Spirit, interpreting spiritual truths to those who possess the Spirit. (1 Cor. 2:10–13)

The fundamental error of some exegetical reductionists, like the Jesus Seminar people, is to deny or ignore this "pneumatological" context of Christological development.

As the Christ Event itself is God's supernatural intervention in history, so its explication and proclamation can only also be a divine action in the Church. It is all the work of the Holy Spirit.

2. There is absolute continuity between the pre-paschal and post-paschal Jesus.

The early Church, with the help of the Holy Spirit, is now confessing and expressing with clarity what was already present in the earthly, historical Jesus but which could not be fully comprehended before the Resurrection or Pentecost.

It is the same Jesus of Nazareth who exercised his ministry in Galilee and Judaea who is now recognized and proclaimed in his full messianic and divine dignity. The Church is not creating a new reality with its post-Pentecost proclamation — but only making more explicit what was already implicit in Jesus' earthly ministry.

This development from an implicit to an explicit Christology was necessitated because:

- Jesus' earthly mission was primarily to reveal the Father and proclaim the Kingdom.
- His self-emptying (*kenosis*) deliberately hid his glory during his earthly life.
- He did not wish to threaten Israel's monotheism.

Yet, the extraordinary teaching, actions, and claims of the pre-paschal Jesus led logically to the early Church's explicit understanding and proclamation of him as Lord. In this development, there is perfect continuity — it is the one and same Jesus who is being confessed. Now, after Easter, his full mystery and dignity are just more clearly understood.

Easter Christology

The Father's raising of Jesus from the dead on Easter Sunday ratifies and authenticates his earthly life and mission. For this reason the early Church's first Christological proclamation was very much focused on the Easter experience.

This first stage of Christological expression was a functional Christology centered on the events of the resurrection and glorification of the Crucified Jesus and on what the Exalted Jesus was now doing in his Church. This early Christology was expressed in Peter's sermon:

> This Jesus God raised up . . . exalted at the right hand of God, and having received from the Father the promise of the Holy Spirit, he has poured out this which you see and hear. . . . Let all the house of Israel therefore know assuredly that God has made him both Lord and Christ, this Jesus whom you crucified. (Acts 2:32–36)

The resurrection of Jesus and the outpouring of the Spirit are the final saving works of God and the definitive inauguration of the Kingdom of God that Jesus had preached. In the Risen Jesus, God has triumphed over sin, evil, and death. This was the essential thrust of the first Christology, and it is called functional Christology because the emphasis is more on what Jesus has done than on the hidden mystery of his person.

Easter Christology is a dynamic one — acknowledging Jesus of Nazareth now as Victor. The victim has become the victor! This is expressed well in the book of Revelation:

I died, and behold I am alive for evermore, and I have the keys of Death and Hades. (Rev. 1:18)

Parousia Christology

The early Church, however, never lost sight of another key aspect of Jesus' mystery — the truth that he would return in glory to complete God's saving work for the human family. This glorious return was called by the Greek word *Parousia*.

In the first written document of Christianity, Paul's letter to the Thessalonians, we find these functional Easter and *Parousia* Christologies fused together:

You turned to God from idols, to serve a living and true God, and wait for his Son from heaven, whom he raised from the dead, Jesus who delivers us from the wrath to come. (1 Thess. 1:9–10)

In its prayer and worship, the earliest community expresses its longing and expectation of this further realization of Christ's saving work. Its often repeated prayer was, "Come, Lord Jesus" (Rev. 22:20; see also 1 Cor. 16:23).

From these Easter and *Parousia* Christologies, the Church developed further in its understanding of Jesus. A sign of the Spirit's presence in the process is the remarkable harmony and unity of the Christological faith expressed in various communities scattered throughout the Middle East who lacked the kind of communication means we take for granted.

This teaching and proclamation was done by unlettered men and women without academic credentials in a hostile environment. Yet, even though different aspects of the mystery of Christ and different titles were used in different churches, there is no contradiction or conflict — rather a harmonious, unified process of worship and proclamation of Jesus as the unique Saving Lord through whom God had accomplished the victory over evil, sin, and death.

Binitarian Worship

What is most noteworthy in the context of the strict Jewish monotheistic setting of early Christianity is how quickly and naturally Jesus of Nazareth became an object of cult and devotion. Larry Hurtado expresses it well:

> The most striking innovation in earliest Christian circles was to include Christ with God as recipient of cultic devotion. What could have prompted such a major innovation in the devotional scruples and practices that were inherited from the Jewish tradition? What might have moved Christian Jews to feel free to offer to Christ this unparalleled cultic devotion? In light of the characteristic reluctance of devout Jews to accord cultic reverence to any figure other than God, it seems likely that those very early circles who took the step of according Christ such reverence could have done so only if they felt compelled by God.[1]

Hurtado notes that this monotheistic context prevented the *apotheosis* of Jesus as a new deity in his own right as pagans would have done, but rather it produced a "binitarian variant" of monotheism in which worship of Jesus always unites him closely to God the Father. This ultimately led to the Johannine passages that most clearly assert both Jesus' true and full divinity but also his oneness in essence with the Father:

I and the Father are one. (Jn. 10:30)

The Father is in me and I in the Father. (Jn. 10:38)

The Father judges no one, but has given all judgment to the Son, that all may honor the Son, even as they honor the Father. (Jn. 5:22–33)

These biblical assertions would be the basis of the Church's later dogmas of the "consubstantiality" between the Father and the Son — that they both share one divine nature. Though Jesus is fully divine, there are not two gods.

Pauline Christology

The Pauline writings are the earliest Christian written sources, and in them already this Jesus worship is highly developed, reflecting the faith of the early Church. We can only briefly outline his teaching. What he taught and wrote was in harmony with the earliest apostolic community.

Paul was very scrupulous about his unity of faith with the most primitive Apostolic church of Jerusalem and the Apostles themselves. He went there twice. He says in

Galatians that "I laid before them . . . the gospel which I preach among the Gentiles, lest somehow I should be running or had run in vain" (Gal. 2:2).

Paul, in his writings, uses two titles that express his Christology and that of the earliest Church: Son of God and Lord.

Son of God

Jesus' divine sonship is the distinguishing mark of Christianity and is rooted already in Jesus' own unique filial consciousness, and in his use of the familiar "Abba" in praying to the Father. Jesus' sonship is a natural sonship so that he is of the same divine nature as the Father. It is radically different from our adoptive sonship as Paul makes clear:

When the time had fully come, God sent forth his Son, born of woman, born under the law, so that we might receive adoption as sons. (Gal. 4:4–5)

Related to Jesus' divine sonship is his pre-existence before the Incarnation. In Paul's theology, there is "a voluntary act on the part of the Son prior to his incarnation. The one who was in the form of God and equal to God empties himself (Phil. 2:6–7), the one who was rich becomes poor for our sake (2 Cor. 8:9)."[2]

Lord

This title reflects Jesus' relationship to us. The adoption of this title by the earliest Christians for Jesus is a striking expression of their faith in his divinity. The Greek word *Kurios* was used in the Greek Scriptures for Yahweh alone.

To now transfer it to Jesus was an exceptional act of faith for these earliest Christians. Paul expresses it dramatically, apparently citing an early Christian hymn:

> God has highly exalted him and bestowed on him the name which is above every name, that at the name of Jesus every knee should bow, in heaven and on earth and under the earth, and every tongue confess that Jesus Christ is Lord, to the glory of God the Father. (Phil. 2:9–10)

In Paul, this title too reminds us of Jesus' pre-existent state and of how he shared with the Father a creative role:

> For us there is one God, the Father, from whom are all things and for whom we exist, and one Lord, Jesus Christ, through whom are all things and through whom we exist. (1 Cor. 8:6)

One scholar has underlined the radical nature of this application of the title "Lord" to Jesus:

> Paul even split the Jewish confession of monotheism in the Shema (Deut. 6:4–5), glossing "God" with Father and "Lord" with Jesus Christ to put Jesus as Lord alongside God the Father.... Here the title "one Lord" expanded the Shema to contain Jesus. Using the classic monotheistic text of Judaism, Paul recast his perception of God by introducing Jesus as "Lord" and redefining Jewish monotheism to produce a christological monotheism.[3]

For all these reasons, confession of Jesus precisely as "Lord" becomes the touchstone of Christian orthodoxy for Paul:

> If you confess with your lips that Jesus is Lord and believe in your heart that God raised him from the dead, you will be saved. (Rom. 10:9)

Synoptic Christology

The Gospels of Mark, Matthew, and Luke reflect the faith in Christ of the early Church that we have just described. They integrate the memories and stories of Jesus in the oral traditions of the community with the clearer faith produced by the Resurrection and the work of the Holy Spirit. Each evangelist has his own particular slant on the mystery of Christ as he adapted it to the issues and needs of his particular community. The reader is encouraged to consult the many Bible commentaries for a full elaboration of each Gospel's approach. Here, in a brief synthetic way, we shall note each one's basic Christological approach:

Mark

Mark focuses his attention on Jesus as Son of God. He begins and ends his Gospel with this title. However, Mark's preoccupation is to emphasize that he came in the form of a humble, obedient, suffering servant: "The Son of Man also came not to be served but to serve, and to give his life as a ransom for many" (Mk. 10:45).

Matthew

This Gospel often reflects a Jewish-oriented Christology. Jesus is the new Moses, miraculously saved like Moses (Mt. 2:13–18). He gives a new law to refine the law of Moses (Mt. 5). He is hailed as the Messiah whom the Jews expect (Mt. 16:16). Given the Jewish context, it is striking that Matthew also emphasizes Jesus' intimate relationship with the Father: "All things have been delivered to me by my Father; and no one knows the Son except the Father, and no one knows the Father except the Son and any one to whom the Son chooses to reveal him" (Mt. 11:27).

Luke

We could say his portrait of Jesus is best summed up in the title Savior. This title he uses already in his nativity account (Lk. 2:11). Luke emphasizes Jesus' compassion, mercy, and receptivity to sinners, women, and the outcasts. Luke organizes the final stage of Jesus' saving ministry around his journey to Jerusalem, where he would demonstrate his role as Savior. Significantly, Luke's Gospel contains Jesus' most merciful words from the cross: "Father, forgive them; for they know not what they do" (Lk. 23:34), and to the good thief crucified with him, "Truly, I say to you, today you will be with me in Paradise" (Lk. 23:43).

Johannine Christology

Perhaps the most fully-developed Christology of the New Testament is found in John's Gospel, whose redaction comes after many decades of the Church's life and of preaching, worship, and contemplation. John's Gospel reflects this rich ecclesial experience and presents the most profound insights into the full mystery of Christ.

A significant Christological aspect of John's Gospel is his use of the title "Word" for the pre-existing Son and his strong union of the idea of divine pre-existence and true Incarnation: "The Word became flesh" (Jn. 1:14). This concept of the Word could come from the Jewish Wisdom tradition, which already had the concept of some mysterious entity that existed with God before creation and was his partner in the creation of the world (e.g., Wis. 7:24ff; Sir. 24; Prov. 8:22ff).

John unites this figure with the Church's understanding of the Eternal Son, and significantly he changes the feminine Sophia of the Old Testament to the masculine Logos.

John emphasizes the communion of life and action between Jesus and the Father. Jesus' miracles are "the Father's works." Jesus is destined to exercise judgment in the Father's name and bring the dead to life, sharing fully the omnipotent power of the Father. Jesus' saving mission is a supreme visible act of love, revealing to the world the inner mystery of the love of the Trinity: "That the world may know that I love the Father" (Jn. 14:31).

Jesus intends to "glorify" the Father by his whole mission and especially by his salvific death (Jn. 12:23–28).

In John's Gospel, the full development of New Testament Christology comes to its necessary conclusion. Instead of the word "God," more and more the language is "Father and Son." The Trinitarian mystery is fully and explicitly proclaimed.

Endnotes — Chapter 6

[1] Larry Hurtado, *Lord Jesus Christ: Devotion to Jesus in Earliest Christianity* (Grand Rapids, MI: Eerdmans, 2003), p. 72.

[2] Roch Kereszty, *Jesus Christ: Fundamentals of Christology* (New York: Alba House, 2002), p. 179.

[3] Gerald O'Collins, *Christology: A Biblical, Historical, and Systematic Study of Jesus* (New York: Oxford University Press, 1995), p. 137.

CHAPTER 7

A DYNAMIC TRADITION

Some Christians, adopting a position of *Sola Scriptura* — "Only Scripture" — wish to terminate Christological reflection with the completion of the written Scriptures. This was not what actually happened in the earliest Church and it is not the faith or practice of the Catholic Church.

The Bible, as we noted in chapter 2, is an ecclesial (church) document. Its content was decided upon by the bishops of the Church at various times in Councils, and by the fourth century the twenty-seven books of the New Testament were universally accepted as canonical (authoritative), and some other writings that existed at the time were not included. These others were well-known at the time and even influenced liturgical practice (e.g., the Gospel of James); other were products of break-off dissident groups such as the Gnostics (e.g., the Gospel of Judas). The Church, however, established the twenty-seven books as inspired Scriptures on an equal level with the Old Testament books.

Christological devotion and reflection continued in these early centuries after the writing of the New Testament books. The center of the preaching and worship of the Church was Jesus, the Crucified and Risen Lord. This new Christian faith had to be preached in the midst of a bewildering multitude of ancient religions, philosophies, and cults. Christian pastors had to interact with their surroundings and defend and explain the new Christian faith to outsiders. As time went on, moreover, questions arose within the community of faith itself, about the mystery of Christ and the Trinity. The human intellect is a restless faculty that is constantly probing and questioning.

Catholic faith has always believed that there is in the Church a dynamism of tradition that is directed by the Holy Spirit. This tradition flows from the same faith that inspired the Scriptures, and it further elucidates and develops the truth in the Scriptures.

The Church has definitively expressed its consciousness and belief in this process in the Second Vatican Council's Dogmatic Constitution on Revelation:

> This tradition which comes from the Apostles develops in the Church with the help of the Holy Spirit. For there is a growth in the understanding of the realities and the words which have been handed down. This happens through the contemplation and study made by believers, who treasure these things in their hearts (see Lk. 2:19, 51) through a penetrating understanding of the spiritual realities which they experience, and through the preaching of those who have received through episcopal succession the sure gift of truth. For as the centuries succeed one another, the Church constantly moves forward

toward the fullness of divine truth until the words of God reach their complete fulfillment in her. (*Dei Verbum*, 8)

One Catholic theologian, Bernard Lonergan, describes one dimension of this important process in philosophical, analytical terms.[1] He observes that there are two kinds of human consciousness:

- **Undifferentiated:** Characterized by a narrative or story-telling style, appealing to the whole person — emotion, intellect, heart, and will. This is the form that most of the New Testament is expressed in because those writings were evangelistic and catechetical documents inviting persons to faith and commitment.
- **Differentiated:** Characterized by a more sober intellectual analysis of the truths proclaimed. This often means analyzing the dialectic dimension of contrasting truth. Obviously, it is precisely this kind of consciousness that was at work when the early Church had to deal with such issues as the humanity and divinity of Jesus, the Oneness and Threeness of God.

This dynamic tradition, this movement from an undifferentiated consciousness to a more differentiated consciousness results in what is called "doctrinal develpment" and ultimately in the formation of dogmas — concise normative expressions of the Church's faith. This was a process, led by the Holy Spirit, that the early Church went through in the first centuries of her existence seeking to ever more carefully proclaim and protect the Apostolic faith in Jesus Christ that she had received.

As we noted earlier in this chapter, this process of development was influenced by the milieu in which the Church was carrying out her mission. It was often in direct response to some challenges that contemporary philosophies posed to the correct understanding of the faith. Many of these philosophies attempted to interpret Christian faith according to their own presuppositions (e.g., Platonic, Gnostic, Docetic).

The Church's response, enunciated by the early bishops and Fathers of the Church, was not primarily philosophical or theoretical, but motivated by the desire to preserve the inherited faith. At its core, this faith proclaimed that it was precisely because the Eternal Son of God assumed a true and full human nature that he was able to effect the salvation of the human race. This central truth had to be defended against all systems that would threaten either the true humanity or true divinity of Christ. As noted earlier, Christology and Soteriology are always intimately linked.

Recent news stories have attempted to sensationalize some of the post–New Testament writings that these Fathers already knew well and dealt with at the time (e.g., the Gospel of Judas). The Fathers pointed out that these writings were produced long after the New Testament period and by authors who had an agenda to promote what was in fact not in harmony with the faith transmitted by the Apostles.

It would be impossible here to adequately treat the complex development of Christological doctrine over the first four centuries. This process took place in both the Greek-speaking world and the Latin-speaking world, over the whole Mediterranean region, and involved many theories and disputes over correct terminology.[2]

It is perhaps a tribute to those times that matters of doctrinal faith were taken so seriously and could engage learned persons and church communities so seriously. They clearly understood that what was ultimately at stake was the truth of human salvation effected in and through Jesus Christ, the Incarnate Son of God and Universal Savior. For this reason, they wanted, in our jargon, "to get it right."

In a very summary fashion, we shall trace this Christological development as it dealt with four key issues and finally was definitively expressed in Ecumenical Councils by the then undivided Church.

Four Christological Issues

1. Full Humanity of Jesus

The very dominant Platonistic philosophy of that period had a negative view of the human body. According to that philosophy, the goal of life was to liberate oneself from the bodily passions and to live in the realm of the spirit. Obviously, the doctrine of Jesus' true and full humanity was a problem for such thinkers.

This faith challenge was already apparent in New Testament times as reflected in John's Epistles:

> Every spirit which confesses that Jesus Christ has come in the flesh is of God, and every spirit which does not confess Jesus is not of God. This is the spirit of antichrist. (1 Jn. 4:2–3)

Heretics known as Docetists taught that Jesus only appeared to be human (from the Greek word for appear, *dokein*). The Fathers, beginning with St. Ignatius of Antioch (d. A.D. 110), vigorously combated this error, asserting the truth of Jesus' full and true humanity. They did so because they knew that Jesus' true human suffering and death are the means of salvation for the human race.

St. Ignatius wrote:

> Turn a deaf ear when anyone speaks to you apart from Jesus Christ, who was of the family of David and Mary, who was truly born, who ate and drank, was truly persecuted under Pontius Pilate, was truly crucified and died, who also was truly raised from the dead. (*Letter to Trallians*, 9, 1).[3]

An important consequence of this strong faith in the true Incarnation was a clear faith in the Eucharistic presence of Christ's body. Accordingly, Ignatius also writes, "I desire the bread of God which is the flesh of Jesus Christ, who was of the seed of David, and for drink I desire his blood, which is love incorruptible" (*Letter to Romans*, 7, 3).

St. Irenaus of Lyons (A.D. 140–202) also wrote extensively against those who denied Christ's true humanity in his work, *Against Heresies*:

> In all things he is man . . . recapitulating man in himself, the invisible is made visible, the incomprehensible is made comprehensible, and that which is not subject to suffering is made subject to suffering.

The Word, becoming man, recapitulates all things
in himself. (Book 3:16, 6)

2. Full Divinity of Jesus

Just as some had denied the humanity of Jesus, others
denied his true divinity. The denial of this central truth
reached a peak in the fourth century in the teaçhings of an
African priest-theologian named Arius who could not reconcile Jesus' divine sonship with his view of monotheism and
the doctrines of the impassibility and unchangeableness of
God.

Arius taught that the Father is absolutely beyond the
Son and, being unbegotten, is the only true God. He
asserted that the Son was not co-eternal — "there was a time
when he was not." In effect, he was making the Son a creature. The great Bishop of Alexandria, St. Athanasius, tartly
responded, "We do not worship a creature." From the beginning of Christianity, Jesus had been the object of worship
and devotion along with the Father.

Arius' ideas had a wide circulation and some support
from the political powers of that time who exercised considerable influence in Church affairs. The reaction of the
Church culminated in the Council of Nicea (A.D. 325).
The Council teaching made a useful and important distinction between "creation" and "generation" as regards
the Divine Son. In words we still use every Sunday in the
Nicene Creed at Mass, it asserted that Jesus "was gener-
ated, not made" from the Father from all eternity. He is
the true Eternal Son of the very same divine nature as his
Father and therefore consubstantial with him.

The Son is not created but begotten by the Father — he is the only begotten Son and of the divine "substance." The Son participates fully in the divine essence, and therefore the Council defined, as we pray each Sunday, that he is "God from God."

This Council and its definitions were a necessary leap beyond biblical language. The bishops of the Council, moved by the Holy Spirit, had to protect and clarify the faith contained in the Scriptures. To do this, they needed to use terms and concepts intelligible to the people of their day. In a certain sense, one could say that with the Council of Nicea "dogma is born."

The dynamic tradition of faith, of which we spoke earlier, continues in the Church in these conciliar teachings. Yet, other aspects still needed to be clarified, and so we turn to the next dilemma facing the early tradition of the Church.

3. The Relationship of Humanity and Divinity in Jesus

The Church had affirmed both the full and true divinity and humanity of Jesus. The question, then, was how did these two interact with one another? Various efforts to understand and express this mystery ultimately led to "dead ends" of heresy that the Church had to confront.

Still today, the Church speaks of "the mysterious union of the Incarnation" (*Catechism of the Catholic Church*, 470), and so we must not expect to clearly understand this marvelous union of humanity and divinity in Christ, but the Church was and is obliged to protect the Mystery from erroneous efforts at explanation.

A theological trend rooted in the Church of Antioch tended to so emphasize the distinction of human and divine natures in Jesus as to threaten the unity of his person. This tendency reached a climax in the teachings of Nestorious, who so divided the two natures as to assert that Mary was the mother of the human Jesus but not the mother of the divine Jesus. For him, the two natures coexisted only by a sort of conjunction, or moral unity. It was as if Jesus were really two entities.

The community reacted strongly and intuitively that this was not the inherited faith of the Church. Already in prior centuries the popular prayer to Mary, "We take refuge in your protection, O Holy Mother of God," had been used. Clearly, Nestorius' ideas were an innovation and departure from that faith.

A different and contrasting theological trend was expressed by the Church in Alexandria in Egypt which so emphasized the role of the Eternal Word in this "mysterious union" that it seemed to swallow up Jesus' true humanity and overwhelm it. Some taught that Jesus did not have a true human soul but that the Word somehow took its place. This error come to be known as Monophysitism (one being) and deprived the humanity of Jesus of a true role in our salvation — thereby depriving the central mystery of the Incarnation of its meaning.

This diminution of Jesus' humanity threatened the doctrine of salvation. It was precisely by his human obedience, suffering, and death that we were saved. Jesus needed to have full human faculties to exercise this saving rule for his human brother and sisters.

4. The Unity of Jesus

It was therefore necessary to find a way of understanding the operation of the humanity and divinity in Jesus in a way that left both intact but also demonstrated a unity of the two in Jesus.

A helpful role in this discussion was played by the Western theologian Tertullian, who used the Latin word *persona*. In Christ, human and divine nature are united "in one person." There is only one subject who acts in both a human and divine way.

The bishops at the Council of Ephesus in A.D. 431 officially affirmed this unity in Jesus and therefore reaffirmed the title of "Mother of God" for Mary.

The Council of Calcedon in A.D. 451 followed up with a more fulsome and technical exposition inspired by a letter of Pope Leo the Great called the *Tome to Flavian*.

The Council spoke of the one *hypostasis* (person) of Jesus, which had two natures — human and divine. Thus was born the term "the hypostatic union" to describe the unity of humanity and divinity in Jesus. This one person, or subject, was the Eternal Word, or Son. The Council asserted that these two natures exist "without confusion or change, without division or separation."

Thus, the mystery (which remains a mystery!) was protected and preserved from theological assaults that would have compromised the basic truth of salvation in and through Jesus Christ that is the Church's essential "good news."

Conclusion

A Spirit-driven process helped the Church to protect and clarify its Christological faith over these important early centuries. A possible drawback, however, with the focus on the ontological approach to Jesus as one person in two natures was to become too philosophical and abstract and diminish the power of the original "Christ Event" and its true historicity and drama. This danger has been well expressed by one theologian:

> Central to the Christian message is not a doctrine but an event, that of God's personal entry into, and decisive commitment to, history in Jesus Christ. . . . The concrete "story" of Jesus must be rediscovered as the embodiment of the personal commitment and self-communication of God to humankind.[4]

As we shall see in the next chapter, subsequent Christological reflection and devotion deepened the Church's approach to the mystery of Christ and kept its character as the primary saving event alive and dynamic.

Endnotes — Chapter 7

[1] See B. Lonergan, *The Way to Nicea* (London: Darton, Longman & Todd, 1976); For Lonergan's full philosophical context see his book *Insight: A Study of Human Understanding* (New York: Longman, 1958).

[2] For a deeper survey of some of these issues, consult J.N.D. Kelly, *Early Christian Doctrines* (New York: Harper &

Row, 1978), and A. Grillmeier, *Christ in Christian Tradition* (Atlanta: John Knox Press, 1972).

[3] Cited in *The Faith of the Early Fathers*, edited by W. Jurges (Collegeville, MN: Liturgical Press, 1970), p.21.

[4] Jacques Dupuis, *Who Do You Say I Am* (New York: Orbis Books, 1994), p. 106.

CHAPTER 8

FELLOWSHIP WITH CHRIST

Though the great Councils of the fourth and fifth centuries brought a dogmatic closure to certain kinds of speculation about the mystery of Christ, the Church's contemplation, worship, and proclamation of him continued, and has to our own time.

St. John uses the beautiful phrase "fellowship" to describe the special relationship of adoration, love, trust, and friendship that every believer is invited to share with the Lord Jesus:

> That which we have seen and heard we proclaim also to you, so that you may have fellowship with us; and our fellowship is with the Father and with his Son Jesus Christ. (1 Jn. 1:3)

This fellowship has been expressed over the centuries in many beautiful and significant ways revealing the inexhaustible riches of the mystery of Christ. In this chapter, we will briefly highlight a few of these expressions based on the prayers and teachings of a few key figures in the Catholic tradition. In fact, perhaps one of the best ways to capture this unfolding Christological faith and devotion is through the prayers addressed to Christ over the centuries by the saints.[1]

The unfolding tradition, however, also dealt with some theological questions and issues in Christology that earlier centuries had not fully engaged. In a very summary way in this chapter, we propose to examine both some of these issues and the devotional approaches of a few key figures.

Augustine of Hippo (A.D. 354–430)

This great bishop of North African origin went through a long and tortuous conversion process both morally and intellectually, which he describes in his *Confessions*. Finally, through the pastoral care of the saintly bishop of Milan, Ambrose, he was baptized and thereafter became a priest and bishop back in North Africa where he had to deal with many challenges to the faith.

First of all, Augustine gives us the proper spiritual dispositions for seeking Jesus. After years of sophisticated dabbling in Neoplatonism and Manichean dualism, he admitted, "I sought with pride what only humility could find."

> You (God) wanted to show me how you oppose the proud but give grace to the humble (see 1 Pet. 5:5), and with what mercy you have shown humanity the way of humility in that your "Word became flesh and dwelt among us" (Jn. 1:14). (*Confessions*: VII, IX, 13)

Further, Augustine came to realize that all his exertions in philosophy seeking to know and understand the nature of God were of limited value:

I tried to find a way of gaining the strength neces-
sary for enjoying You and I could not find it until I
embraced that Mediator between God and men
(Jesus) who was calling to me and saying, "I am the
Way, the Truth, and the Life." (*Confessions*: VII,
XVIII, 24)

Augustine came to see in a very personal way the mediating role of Jesus between searching men and the transcendent God. Christ is the only bridge over the infinite chasm
that separates us from God.

As one patristic scholar has explained:

One title of Christ that remains dominant throughout Augustine's work is Mediator. This term had the
advantage of being both biblical — the New Testament speaks of Christ as the "one mediator between
God and men" (1 Tim. 2:5) and congenial to the
Neoplatonic conception of a universe held together
by divine energy that radiates outward from the single center through levels of decreasing reality and
goodness. . . . (citing Augustine) "Therefore, he is
the Mediator between God and humanity because
he is God with the Father, because he is human
among human beings. Divinity without humanity
is not a mediator, humanity without divinity is not
a mediator; but between divinity alone and humanity alone, the mediating link is the human divinity
and the divine humanity of Christ."[2]

Augustine's focus on Jesus as Mediator is timely in our moment of history. Many persons superficially, if not arrogantly, assert they can have their own direct relationship with the Transcendent God. They are impatient or intolerant of structures or sacraments that might be deemed necessary roads to communion with God. In fact, we can have no real communion with God except through Christ in whom God stoops to us. He is the necessary mediator and his mediation is perpetuated in the structures (Church) and sacraments through which he has chosen to continue his mediating and saving role. These truths were powerfully restated by the Church at the Second Vatican Council in the Dogmatic Constitution on the Church, *Lumen Gentium*.

Anselm of Canterbury (1033–1109)

Anselm, a Benedictine monk and abbot of the fervent Abbey of Bec in Normandy, become Archbishop of Canterbury in England. His book, *Cur Deus Homo* (Why God Became Man), had a significant influence on subsequent Christology. He sought to determine the need for the Incarnation of the Son of God.

He found his answer in the reality of sin and in the dialectic between God's mercy and justice. He sees sin as an offense against God who is Infinite, and therefore the offense is infinite. God is Merciful but cannot forgive men without "satisfaction." Humans are unable to make this satisfaction because their actions are only finite. The sinner owes God something greater than he can pay.

Only God can give God something worthy of himself. The solution for this dialectic for Anselm was the saving Incarnation. The Son, true God, but also man, would, by his suffering and death, offer the Father a sacrifice capable of satisfying divine justice. Jesus become the representative of sinful humanity in paying the price justice required.

Some have suggested that Anselm found germs of this idea in the Rule of St. Benedict with which he would have been very familiar as a monk. The Rule deals with moral faults and satisfaction that should be made to atone for them.[3]

Whatever the source of his insight, Anselm's theory does seem to harmonize significantly with the teaching of Paul:

For our sake he made him to be sin who knew no sin, so that in him we might become the righteousness of God. (2 Cor. 5:21)

Anselm's teaching casts light on the truth that Jesus is indeed the Savior. In our moment of history in which sin is so often trivialized, Anselm's insight is a helpful reminder of the ultimate evil, which is sin.

Some theologians make a helpful objection or correction to this theory of "representative satisfaction," noting that it concentrates too narrowly on the cross and doesn't adequately account for the whole of the Christ Event. This seems like a legitimate point that does not, however, erase the value of Anselm's insight and contribution. It is crucial to see the saving value of the Incarnation itself and of the whole Christ Event.

Bernard of Clairvaux (1090–1153)

Bernard, a Cistercian monk and abbot, preached and wrote frequently about Jesus. His writings project a deep apprecia-

tion of the sacred humanity of Jesus. He also expresses a contemplative sense of intimate familiarity with the Lord. These
sentiments are expressed in his hymn to Christ:

> O Jesus — to think of you is sweet
> Giving true joy to the heart but
> sweeter than all else will be your presence
>
> No song is sweeter,
> no word more delightful
> no thought more pleasing
> than of Jesus, God's Son
>
> Jesus, hope of penitents
> how loving to those who seek you
> how good to them who implore you;
> but what joy to those who find you!
>
> O Jesus, be our joy now,
> who are to be our great reward;
> May all our glory be in you
> Now and forever

(Author's translation)

If Anselm had a deep understanding of Jesus as victim of
divine justice, Bernard had a sense of Jesus' merciful love for
those for whom he died — a love that should inspire bound-
less trust and confidence. He wrote in one of his sermons:

> Through his sacred wounds we can see the secret of
> his heart... where have your love, your mercy, your

compassion shone out more luminously than in your wounds, sweet, gentle Lord of Mercy? My merit comes from his mercy. Even if I am aware of many sins, what does it matter? Where sin abounded grace has overflowed. (*Sermon on the Song of Songs*, 61, 3–5)

Bernard also sees the various stages of Jesus' earthly life as both models for his disciples and sources of grace for spiritual growth. Our personal appropriation of Jesus' virtues become a path of holiness. In this sense, in Bernard, there is a transition from focus on "objective redemption" to "subjective redemption" — how all of Christ's mysteries bear fruit in us. This approach would be brought to a rich development in the twentieth century by another monk — Blessed Columba Marmion.[4]

Francis of Assisi (1181–1226)

Many believe that Francis was the person who most perfectly captured the ideal of assimilation of Christian virtues in his own life. His poverty, humility, and loving service radiated the virtues of Jesus to the people of his time and sparked a religious revival embodied in the many Franciscan communities that sprang from his inspiration.

Francis also first introduced the custom of the Christmas Crèche, or manger scene, as a way of capturing the reality of that event of salvation. The famous Cross of San Damiano, which spoke to Francis during prayer, symbolized his great devotion to the mystery of the Cross.

Francis' Christ-centered spirituality was crowned by a special configuration to Christ's passion. In 1224, while devoting extended time to prayer on the summit of Monte

La Verna, his body received the marks of Christ's Passion —
nail prints on his hands and feet and a wound in his side.

His preaching and his example, united to that of his
followers, forms an essential component of the
Christocentric spirituality of the medieval period
that still lives in the devotion of the Christian
people.[5]

St. Thomas Aquinas (1225–1224)

This brilliant Dominican friar theologian systematized much
of Catholic theology, especially in his *Summa Theologica*. He
took elements of the patristic and medieval traditions and
reshaped them.

The foundation of Thomas' Christology (contained in
the *Summa*, Part Three, Questions 1–59) is the ancient conciliar teaching on the hypostatic union of Christ's divine
and human natures in one person.

From this point of view, it is very much Christology
"from above." The eternal Person of the Word has taken on
a human nature to be the Savior. Because of this union, his
whole life was salvific and had infinite value. Yet Thomas
goes beyond the Anselmian strict justice approach when he
notes about mankind's sin: "The offense is cancelled only by
love" (*Contra Gentiles*, 3:157). It is Christ's love that makes
the satisfaction efficacious, not just his divine status.

Some theologians would argue that Thomas' approach
regarding the effect of the hypostatic union on Jesus greatly
diminished the reality of his human nature:

Aquinas encouraged the subsequent Catholic theological tradition to hold that in his human mind the earthly Jesus enjoyed the beatific vision and hence lived by sight not by faith. Notable difficulties can be brought against this view. For instance, the comprehensive grasp of all creatures and all they can do (which Aquinas attributed to the beatific vision) would lift Christ's human knowledge so clearly beyond the normal limits as to cast serious doubts on the genuiness of his humanity, at least in one essential aspect.[6]

Ignatius of Loyola (1491–1556)

Ignatius, the founder of the Jesuit order, was not a speculative theologian, but more of a brilliant spiritual guide. His system was expressed in the *Spiritual Exercises*, which are totally Christocentric. His goal was to help persons to make a very concrete and definitive choice to follow Christ the King and to order their lives in his service.

To inspire this ideal, he leads those who follow the *Exercises* through a series of contemplations of the various mysteries of Christ so that the power and grace of each of these revelations of his mystery may become personal and effective for the retreatants.

The ultimate desired disposition of the true disciple of Christ is one of self-abandonment and total availability for the cause of Christ. Ignatius expresses this well in this prayer to Jesus:

Take, Lord and receive all my liberty, my memory, my understanding, and all my will — all that I have and possess, you, Lord, have given to me, I now give it back to you, O Lord. All of it is yours. Dispose of me according to your will. Give me love of yourself along with your grace, for that is enough for me!

St. John Eudes (d. 1680)
St. Margaret Mary Alacoque (d. 1690)

In a period that was infected by the rigorist Jansenistic doctrine that overemphasized the sinfulness of man to a point that seemed to bar hope or access to Christ, devotion to the loving and merciful Sacred Heart of Jesus emerged, inspired especially by these two saints.

St John Eudes' devotion is expressed in his prayer:

O Jesus, my Lord, I surrender myself to the might of Your divine spirit and your holy love in their immense power and greatness; I adore, glorify, and love you in Yourself and in all the mysteries and phases of your life.

St. Margaret Mary was a cloistered Visitation nun in France who received a series of apparitions of Christ during 1675. To her Jesus said, "Behold the heart which has so loved men that it has spared nothing!"

St. Margaret Mary saw the heart of Christ — with flames of love coming from it, circled by thorns, and showing the wound made by the spear on Good Friday. This symbol became a powerful icon of the merciful love of Christ, and devotion to the Sacred Heart spread widely.

This devotion was especially characterized by the observance of the First Fridays of nine months as days of special devotion and reparation to the Sacred Heart, and by enthronement of the picture of the Sacred Heart in homes. Finally, the Church established the Feast of the Sacred Heart of Jesus to be observed in the Universal Church on the Friday after Corpus Christi.

> In the mind of St. John Eudes and St. Margaret Mary Alacoque, devotion to the Sacred Heart was intended to express an authentic cult to the love of God towards men which was concretized in the redemptive mystery of the Son of God Incarnate.[7]

St. Faustina Kowalska (1905–1938)

Very much in the spirit of St. Margaret Mary, this young Polish nun was also favored with a series of visions of Christ in which he renewed to her the truth of his divine mercy and asked that an image reflecting this truth be created with rays coming from his heart reflecting the blood and water that flowed from his pierced side on Calvary. Christ asked Faustina "to proclaim that mercy is the greatest attribute of God." He urged that the first Sunday after Easter be observed as Divine Mercy Sunday and urged the frequent repetition of the prayer, "Jesus, I trust in you."[8]

A young Polish Bishop, Karol Wojtyla, promoted the cause of Sister Faustina and the devotion to Jesus as Divine Mercy. In October 1978, the young bishop became pope and eventually would issue an Encyclical Letter — *Dives in Misericordia* — *Rich in Mercy*, canonize St. Faustina, and established Divine Mercy Sunday.

In one revelation, Jesus said to Faustina:

My mercy is so great that no mind, be it of man or
of angel, will be able to fathom it throughout all
eternity. Anything that exists has come forth from
the very depths of my most tender mercy. Every soul
in its relation to me will contemplate my love and
mercy throughout eternity.[9]

Sr. Faustina died of tuberculosis after a long and painful
illness but her legacy of devotion to the Merciful Christ has
spread widely.

Teilhard de Chardin (1881–1955)

Father de Chardin was a French Jesuit trained in the natural sciences, especially geology and paleontology. He spent
much time in China on scientific expeditions and died in
New York City.

Teilhard saw no opposition between science and faith
and attempted in his writings to bridge the gap that some
had imagined after the scientific revolution of the two pre-
ceding centuries. He was especially taken by Darwin's evolutionary theories.

De Chardin embraced and extended Darwin's key
insights (on evolution) by interpreting in the key of
evolution the whole cosmological and human story
from creation to the final consummation. His scheme
of cosmogenesis , anthropogenesis , and Christogen-
esis detected an evolving spiritualization of matter,
in which humanity and the entire universe move
towards the final consummation in Christ as the
omega-point. Teilhard's evolutionary Christology rec-

ognized Christ as the intrinsic goal and purpose of the entire cosmic-historical evolution.[10]

Although Teilhard's work has some ambiguities, especially regarding the gratuitous nature of the salvation of Christ, his union of the divine work of creation and redemption with a Christ–centered focus is very helpful. In a scientific and empirical culture, it can perhaps help some thinkers see the divine hand in all of reality.

In his Easter Vigil homily of 2006, Pope Benedict XVI spoke in terms that seem consonant with Teilhard's insight:

> Christ's Resurrection is something more, something different than somebody once brought back to life. If we may borrow the language of the theory of evolution, it is the greatest "mutation," absolutely the most crucial leap into a totally new dimension that there has ever been in the long history of life and its development: a leap into a completely new order which concerns us and the whole of history.
>
> The Resurrection was like an explosion of light, an explosion of love which dissolved the hitherto indissoluble compenetration of "dying and becoming." It ushered in a new dimension of being, a new dimension of life in which, in a transformed way, matter too was integrated and through which a new world emerges.
>
> It is a qualitative leap in the history of "evolution" and of life in general towards a new future life, towards a new world which, starting from Christ,

already continuously permeates this world of ours, transforms it and draws it to itself.

Endnotes — Chapter 8

[1] Benedict Groeschel, *Praying to Our Lord Jesus Christ: Prayers and Meditations through the Centuries* (San Francisco: Ignatius Press, 2004).

[2] Brian Daley, "Christology," in *Augustine, An Encyclopedia*, edited by A. Fitzgerald (Grand Rapids, MI: Eardmans, 1999), p. 168.

[3] John Fortin, "Satisfaction in St. Benedict's Rule and St. Anselm's *Cur Deus Homo*," *The Modern Schoolman*, LXXIX, May 2002.

[4] Columba Marmion, O.S.B. See his trilogy, *Christ Life of the Soul*; *Christ in his Mysteries*; and *Christ, Ideal of the Priest*. They present a scriptural and theological exposition of "subjective redemption" from a Christological perspective.

[5] Angelo Amato, *Gesù il Signore* (Bologna: Edizioni Dehoniane, 2003), p. 376.

[6] Gerald O'Collins, *Christology: A Biblical, Historical and Systematic Study of Jesus* (New York: Oxford University Press, 1995), p. 207.

[7] Angelo Amato, *Gesù il Signore* (Bologna: Edizioni Dehoniane, 2003), p. 378.

[8] S. Michalenko, *The Life of Faustina Kowalska* (Ann Arbor: Servant Press, 1999).

[9] Ibid., p. 132.

[10] Gerald O'Collins, *Christology: A Biblical, Historical and Systematic Study of Jesus* (New York: Oxford University Press, 1995), p. 218.

CHAPTER 9

NO OTHER SAVIOR?

Having seen the growth of the Christological tradition over the centuries, we conclude by treating one issue that is a contemporary challenge to the Church's Christological faith and proclamation.

We live in a world that is no longer Eurocentric. Because of modern communications, everyone can be readily aware of the many philosophies and religions of people all over the globe. We are more aware and respectful of the great numbers of people who adhere to other religious faiths.

Moreover, the dominant culture is one characterized, as the current Holy Father has said, by the "tyranny of relativism." Absolute truth is denied. Everyone's opinion or theory is considered of equal value. It is considered impertinent or arrogant to assert that there are objective norms or truths that might be binding on others or normative for all people everywhere.

It is precisely in this double context of global awareness and relativism that the Church repeats her two-thousand-year-old faith about the Lord Jesus: "There is salvation in no one else, for there is no other name under heaven given among men by which we must be saved" (Acts 4:12).

Jesus himself, as we saw in chapter 4, linked the coming of God's Kingdom, and therefore salvation, to his own person. Jesus' Resurrection confirmed this claim, and the first Christians had no doubt about his unique and necessary role. This is the essence of Christianity.

This ancient apostolic teaching was reaffirmed by the Church in an important Declaration of the Congregation for Doctrine, *Dominus Jesus*, on August 6, 2000. Media reports immediately tried to hype the document as a confrontational or polemical attack by the Church on people of other religions. It was, of course, nothing of the sort. It was aimed at the Catholic community and issued as a service especially for the Church in Asia, where some ideas were being circulated by a few Catholic theologians that raised questions about the unique role of Jesus.

Christianity began very conscious of a universal mission — "Go therefore and make disciples of all nations" (Mt. 28:19). From the first, Christians recognized their obligation to witness to and share their faith in Jesus Christ as the one who brought humanity the gift of salvation and eternal life.

These were spiritual goods to which all people had a right, and so from the start the Church had a missionary impetus. This was not motivated by a sense of superiority or triumphalism or a search for power over others. It was rather seen as the ultimate way to enhance human dignity and respond to the deepest yearnings of the human heart.

It is true that others will be brought to faith in Jesus more by witness than by theological argument. Presenting Christ's universal sacrificial love may be the most compelling way of bringing others to faith in him.

The document *Dominus Jesus* restates some traditional Church teaching that, in the modern relativistic context, is very helpful to keep in mind in our own witness to Jesus Christ:

1. A fullness of revelation has occurred through Jesus Christ.

As the Letter to the Hebrews states:

In many and various ways God spoke of old to the fathers by the prophets; but in these last days he has spoken to us by a Son, whom he appointed the heir of all things, through whom also he created the ages. (Heb. 1:1–2)

Corresponding to revelation, God's self-disclosure in Jesus, there is the human response: to accept God's revealed truth. This acceptance is faith — so the Declaration *Dominus Jesus* notes:

The proper response to God's revelation is "the obedience of faith" by which man freely entrusts his entire self to God, offering the full submission of intellect and will to God who reveals and freely assenting to the revelation given by him. (#7)

2. Jesus' unique and irreplaceable role

It is not possible to consider Jesus as one of many possible mediators. He is rather the Eternal Word and Son who took our human nature precisely to atone for sin and reconcile all people to the Father:

> All this is from God, who through Christ reconciled us to himself and gave us the ministry of reconciliation; that is, in Christ God was reconciling the world to himself, not counting their trespasses against them, and entrusting to us the message of reconciliation. . . . For our sake he made him to be sin who knew no sin, so that in him we might become the righteousness of God. (2 Cor. 5:18–19, 21)

Jesus' saving work is definitive and valid for all. God the Father's salvific plan for all humankind is realized in Jesus, and he is the Savior for all people of all time.

What, then, are we to think of the other major religions of the world, such as Islam, Buddhism, and Hinduism? The best answer is the one given by the Second Vatican Council in its Declaration on the Relation of the Church to Non-Christian Religions:

> The Catholic Church rejects nothing that is true and holy in these religions. She regards with sincere reverence those ways of conduct and of life, those precepts and teachings which, though differing in many aspects from the ones she holds and

sets forth, nonetheless often reflect a ray of that Truth which enlightens all men. Indeed, she proclaims, and ever must proclaim Christ "the way, the truth, and the life" (John 14:6). (*Nostra Aetate*, 2)

In ancient times Christianity meant liberation from paganism. As St. Paul wrote to the Thessalonians, in perhaps the first written book of the New Testament:

You turned to God from idols, to serve a living and true God, and to wait for his Son from heaven, whom he raised from the dead, Jesus who delivers us from the wrath to come. (1 Thess. 1:9–10)

Christian life begins with this "turning," this conversion to the true God and a leaving behind of inadequate or erroneous religious systems or philosophies. This conversion is basic and definitive for being a disciple of the Lord Jesus.

What was true 2,000 years ago is no less true today — even though by means of communication we know much more about other religions than did our forebears.

Jesus shines forth as the *lumen gentium* — the "light of all peoples," as Simeon proclaimed as he held the Infant Christ in his arms. He comes for all as a gentle Savior to bring the truth, grace, and hope for which all people yearn and to raise them to the dignity of children of God.

In Jesus, God has acted definitively in this world to show his mercy and love for us. This basic truth of Christianity is precisely what distinguishes it from many of the

world religions — Islam, Buddhism, Hinduism. In many of
these religions God is passive and aloof from the human
drama. In these religions, what is primary is man's effort to
seek out the divine and raise himself by ascesis and detach-
ment to some kind of personal spiritual "enlightenment."

In Christianity, by contrast, God takes the initiative.
God seeks out man and, in Jesus Christ, he shares humanity's earthly destiny. In Christ, God comes to meet and
embrace us, to reconcile us and divinize us. This is why
Jesus is the unique and only Savior, the essential Mediator
between God and the human race.